Guidelines on Requirements and Preparation for ISMS Certification based on ISO/IEC 27001

Guidelines on Requirements and Preparation for ISMS Certification based on ISO/IEC 27001

Edward (Ted) Humphreys

bsi.

First published in the UK in 1999
Second edition 2002
Third edition 2005
Reprinted 2007
Fourth edition 2014
By
BSI Standards Limited
389 Chiswick High Road
London W4 4AL

BIP 0071 replaces DISC PD 3001 and PD 3001 which are withdrawn.

Typeset in Frutiger by Letterpart Limited
Printed in Great Britain by Berforts Group, www.berforts.co.uk
British Library Cataloguing in Publication Data
A catalogue record for this book is available from the British Library

ISBN 978 0 580 82912 3

Contents

Information Security Management Systems Guidance series

The Information Security Management Systems (ISMS) series of books is designed to provide users with assistance on establishing, implementing, maintaining, checking and auditing their ISMS in order to prepare for certification. Titles in this Information Security Management Systems Guidance series include:

- *Guidelines on requirements and preparation for ISMS certification based on ISO/IEC 27001* (ref.: BIP 0071);
- *Are you ready for an ISMS audit based on ISO/IEC 27001?* (ref.: BIP 0072);
- *Guide to the implementation and auditing of ISMS controls based on ISO/IEC 27001* (ref.: BIP 0073);
- *Measuring the effectiveness of your ISMS implementations based on ISO/IEC 27001* (ref.: BIP 0074);
- *Information security risk management — Handbook for ISO/IEC 27001* (ref.: BIP 0076).

Acknowledgements

Special thanks go to Dr Angelika Plate (one of the co-editors of the 2013 edition of ISO/IEC 27001) for her expert opinion and her attentive and detailed review of this guide. Thanks also go to those SC27 ISMS experts who have been consulted during the development of this guide, and to the founder/director and experts of the ISMS International User Group who supplied some of the appropriate background intellectual property.

Foreword

Information is one of your organization's most valuable assets. The objectives of information security are to protect the confidentiality, integrity and availability of information. These basic elements of information security help to ensure that an organization can protect against:

- sensitive or confidential information being given away, leaked or disclosed, both accidentally or in an unauthorized way;
- personally identifiable information being compromised;
- critical information being accidentally or intentionally modified without your knowledge;
- any important business information being lost without trace or hope of recovery;
- any important business information being rendered unavailable when needed.

It should be the responsibility of all managers, information system owners or custodians, and users in general, to ensure that the information they are processing is properly managed and protected from a variety of risks and threats faced by every organization. The two standards, ISO/IEC 27001:2013, *Information technology — Security techniques — Information security management systems — Requirements* and ISO/IEC 27002:2013, *Information technology — Security techniques — Code of practice for information security controls,* together provide a basis for organizations to develop an effective information security management framework for protecting their important business assets, whilst managing their risks, helping to maximize the organization's investments and business opportunities, and ensuring their information systems continue to be available and operational.

ISO/IEC 27001:2013 is the requirements standard that can be used for accredited third-party information security management system (ISMS) certifications. Organizations going through the accredited certification route to obtain an ISMS certificate would need their ISMS to be audited and assessed by an accredited certification body (see section 5 of this guide) to ensure that they have appropriate management processes and systems in place that conform to the requirements specified in the ISO/IEC 27001 ISMS standard.

ISO/IEC 27002:2013, *Information technology — Security techniques — Code of practice for information security controls* provides a comprehensive set of best practice controls for information security and implementation guidance. Organizations can adopt these controls as part of the risk treatment process specified in ISO/IEC 27001:2013 in order to manage the risks they face to their information assets.

This guide, BIP 0071, as with the other guides in the BIP 0070 series, is designed to provide users with assistance in establishing, implementing and maintaining their ISMS to help them in preparing for ISMS certification. This is the fourth edition of this guide and it has been produced to reflect the publication of the new editions of ISO/IEC 27001 and ISO/IEC 27002.

Note: A document such as this is provided with the best of intentions. It reflects common practice that is derived by a consensus among those with a wide variety of skills, knowledge and experience in the subject. This guide makes no claim to be exhaustive or definitive and users of this guide may need to seek further guidance in implementing the requirements of ISO/IEC 27001:2013 or in using the guidance found in ISO/IEC 27002:2013. Furthermore, there will always be other aspects where additional guidance is required relevant to the organizational, operational, legal and environmental context of the business, including specific threats, controls, regulatory compliance, governance and good practice. BSI or the author of this guide cannot be held liable by organizations, users or third parties for any loss or damage, arising directly or indirectly in connection with reliance on the contents of this guide, or in the execution or implementation of this information. It has been assumed in the drafting of the information and advice given in this guide that the execution of this information by organizations and users is entrusted to appropriately qualified and experienced people.

1 General

1.1 Scope of this guide

This document provides guidance and commentary on the requirements specified in the information security management system (ISMS) standard ISO/IEC 27001:2013. It gives guidance on the complete 'life cycle' of ISMS activities required to establish, implement, monitor and continually improve a set of management controls and processes to achieve effective information security.

1.2 Field of application

1.2.1 Usage

This guide is intended to be used by those involved in:

- designing, implementing and maintaining an ISMS;
- preparing for ISMS audits and assessments;
- undertaking ISMS audits and assessments.[1]

The different types of ISMS audits include first-party audits, such as internal ISMS audits, second-party audits, such as those carried out by customer auditors, and third-party audits, such as those carried out by accredited certification bodies.

This guide provides commentary on the implementation of the processes defined in ISO/IEC 27001:2013 to help understand and prepare for third-party ISMS audits to achieve accredited certification against ISO/IEC 27001:2013. It is also useful for those carrying out internal audits on a regular basis or those doing a pre-audit assessment prior to a formal third-party audit.

[1] Auditors deployed by the organization to carry out an internal ISMS audit, auditors from certification bodies and assessors from accreditation bodies engaged in assessing certification bodies.

1.2.2 Compliance

To claim compliance with the requirements in ISO/IEC 27001:2013 the organization needs to demonstrate that it has all the processes in place and needs to provide appropriate objective evidence to support such claims. Any exclusion of controls found to be necessary to satisfy the risk acceptance criteria needs to be justified and evidence needs to be provided that the associated risks have been knowingly and objectively accepted by those in management who have the executive responsibility for making such decisions and who are accountable for making such decisions.

Excluding any of the requirements specified in Clauses 4 to 10 of ISO/IEC 27001:2013 is not acceptable.

The implementation of a set of ISMS processes results in the organization deploying a system of controls based on a risk management approach to manage its risks. The organization should have implemented an effective system of management controls and processes as part of its ISMS, and it should be able to demonstrate this by providing evidence to the ISMS auditor or audit team (whether it be a first, second or third-party audit).

This guide can be used by those who may not have an immediate need for an external ISMS audit but who require an understanding for establishing and implementing ISMS-based or industry-accepted best practice processes. However, claiming compliance with ISO/IEC 27001:2013 does require the organization to have at least an internal ISMS audit in place whether or not it goes for a third-party audit at a later stage. The organization may not have a business case for a third-party audit, but, to be compliant with ISO/IEC 27001:2013, the internal ISMS audit is mandatory. This guide can, of course, also be used by those preparing for a second and third-party audit.

1.3 Definitions

For the purposes of this guide, the definitions listed in ISO/IEC 27000:2012, ISO 31000, ISO/IEC 17000, ISO/IEC 17021:2011, ISO/IEC 27006:2011 and ISO/IEC 27007 apply.

1.4 Related documents

This guide makes reference to the following standards and guidelines:

- BIP 0074, *Measuring the effectiveness of your ISMS implementations based on ISO/IEC 27001*;
- BIP 0076, *Information security risk management — Handbook for ISO/IEC 27001*;

- BS 7799-3:2006, *Information security management systems — Guidelines for information security risk management*;
- IEC/ISO 31010:2009, *Risk management — Risk assessment techniques*;
- ISO 9001, *Quality management systems — Requirements*;
- ISO 19011:2011, *Guidelines for auditing management systems*;
- ISO 31000:2009, *Risk management — Principles and guidelines*;
- ISO/IEC 17000:2004, *Conformity assessment — Vocabulary and general principles*;
- ISO/IEC 17021:2011, *Conformity assessment — Requirements for bodies providing audit and certification of management systems*;
- ISO/IEC 20000-1:2011, *Information technology — Service management — Part 1: Service management system requirements*;
- ISO/IEC 27000:2012, *Information technology — Security techniques — Information security management systems - Overview and vocabulary*;
- ISO/IEC 27001:2013, *Information technology — Security techniques — Information security management systems — Requirements*;
- ISO/IEC 27002:2013, *Information technology — Security techniques — Code of practice for information security controls*;
- ISO/IEC 27004: 2009, *Information technology — Security techniques — Information security management — Measurement*;
- ISO/IEC 27005:2011, *Information technology — Security techniques — Information security risk management*;
- ISO/IEC 27006:2011, *Information technology — Security techniques — Requirements for bodies providing audit and certification of information security management systems*;
- ISO/IEC 27007:2011, *Information technology — Security techniques — Guidelines for information security management systems auditing*;
- ISO/IEC JTC1/SC27 will be publishing the following standard: ISO/IEC JTC 1/SC27/WG1 SD3 - ISO/IEC 27001 and ISO/IEC 27002 'old to new' transition maps. Extracts of this are included in Annex A of this guide;
- ISO/IEC Directives, *Part 1 — Consolidated ISO Supplement — Procedures specific to ISO.*

Note: Users should always ensure that the correct version of these standards is used. The list above indicates the date of publication of the current editions of these standards at the time of the publication of this guide. However, all standards are reviewed from time to time to check their currency and validity, and this can result in a revised edition being published.

This document is one of a set of five guides published by BSI to support the use and application of ISO/IEC 27001:2013 and ISO/IEC 27002:2013. The reader may find it of benefit to have copies of these other guides:

- BIP 0072, *Are you ready for an ISMS audit based on ISO/IEC 27001?*
- BIP 0073, *Guide to the implementation and auditing of ISMS controls based on ISO/IEC 27001*;
- BIP 0074, *Measuring the effectiveness of your ISMS implementations based on ISO/IEC 27001* (also listed above);
- BIP 0076, *Information security risk management — Handbook for ISO/IEC 27001* (also listed above).

2 Essence of information security

2.1 Confidentiality

The information, in any form, while in storage, being processed or communicated, should be protected to ensure it is only available to those who are authorized by the organization and/or its owner to have access to and use of the information.

Many forms of access control are basically about protecting confidentiality. Encryption is another example of a control, which can be used to protect the confidentiality of information. Controls may be applied at every level of an ISMS: at the physical level (e.g. locks on doors, filing cabinets and safes), and at the logical level (e.g. individual data fields in a database, data in applications and data in hard copy form such as paper documents). In every case the threats and vulnerabilities should be identified, the associated risks assessed, and a system of controls selected, implemented and applied to protect against these risks.

2.2 Integrity

Ensuring that information in storage, being processed or communicated is accurate and complete, that it is correctly processed, and that it has not been modified in any unauthorized way. An organization may also wish to establish the integrity of the networks and information systems that it connects to ensure that these are what the organization intends them to be.

Many data-handling devices, including disk drives and other media and telecommunications systems, contain automatic integrity-checking facilities to ensure that they do not corrupt data. Integrity controls are essential in operating systems, software and application programs in order to prevent intentional or unintentional corruption of software and data during processing. Integrity controls need to be included at the procedural level to reduce the risks of human error, theft or fraud, e.g. controls for input/output data validation, user training and other operational-type controls.

2.3 Availability

Ensuring that information is available to the organization and its users who are authorized to have access to it, when and where they need to use and process it.

In practice, the availability of information requires a system of controls, e.g. information backups, capacity planning, procedures and criteria for system acceptance, incident management procedures, management of removable computer media, information-handling procedures, equipment maintenance and testing, procedures for monitoring system use, and business continuity procedures. Monitoring, reviewing and checking security incidents, service levels and system performance in a timely and ongoing manner can be a preventive control to ensure availability.

2.4 Sensitive, critical or personally identifiable information

ISO/IEC 27002:2013 defines a number of controls that apply to the protection of sensitive, critical and/or personally identifiable information. What is sensitive, critical and personally identifiable information and how do we recognize it? The definition will be different for every organization. Some means should be found to assess the value or utility of information in the context of the individual organization in order to be able to label information as sensitive, critical or personally identifiable when needed and the rest as non-sensitive or non-critical (ISO/IEC 27001:2013, Annex A, Clause A.8.2 defines controls for information classification and handling).

There is also a time element related to the protection of information assets: an organization's financial information will be very sensitive in the days before reporting to the stock market, but will have no sensitivity at all once reported. Sensitivity will also be reflected in the level of classification given to the data. Personally identifiable information relating to individual users, employees, customers and clients needs also to be reflected in the level of information protection that is provided.

A key element in protecting sensitive, critical and/or personally identifiable information is to assess the risk to such information and then to apply the right risk treatment to achieve the level of security required to protect these information assets. ISO/IEC 27001 defines a risk assessment process (6.1.2) and a risk treatment process (6.1.3) for this purpose, and Annex A of ISO/IEC 27001 defines a number of appropriate controls for treating the risks.

3 Information security management system (ISMS)

3.1 Introduction

3.1.1 ISMS concept

The fundamental idea behind the ISMS standard ISO/IEC 27001:2013 is to provide requirements for establishing, implementing, maintaining and continually improving an ISMS to achieve effective information security. The ISMS preserves the confidentiality, integrity and availability of information by applying a risk management process and gives confidence to interested parties that risks are adequately managed.

3.1.2 ISMS – a strategic decision

The adoption of an ISMS is a strategic decision for an organization. The organization's needs and objectives, security requirements, the organizational processes used, and the size and structure of the organization influence the establishment and implementation of an organization's ISMS. All of these influencing factors are expected to change over time.

3.1.3 Information security risks

Risks to an organization's information assets are a problem every organization needs to face and to do something about. No organization can operate successfully in today's world without information security to counter these risks. The ISMS should be designed to ensure adequate and proportionate information security management is in place to protect the organization's information assets and to give confidence and assurance to interested parties.

ISO/IEC 27001:2013 includes requirements for the assessment and treatment of information security risks tailored to the internal and external context of the organization, and the needs, expectations and requirements of all relevant interested parties (internal and external). The requirements set out in this international standard are generic and are intended to be applicable to all organizations, regardless of type, size or nature. The 2013 edition of ISO/IEC 27001 has been aligned with ISO 31000 in terms of definitions, terminology and principles.

3.1.4 Integrated approach

It is important that the ISMS activities are implemented as an integral part of the organization's overall management structure. For information security risk management to be relevant to the organization it should be embedded in the organization's culture and practices, and tailored to the business processes of the organization in order to be appropriate, effective and efficient.

Information security should be considered in the design of business processes, information systems and controls. The flexible nature of any ISO/IEC 27001:2013 ISMS implementation means that it can be scaled and customized in accordance with the needs of the organization.

3.1.5 Risk management principles

In considering information security risk management it is useful to consider the best practice risk management principles outlined in ISO 31000 as a basis for ISO/IEC 27001 ISMS risk management:

a) Risk management creates and protects value.
Risk management contributes to the demonstrable achievement of objectives and improvement of performance in, for example, human health and safety, security, legal and regulatory compliance, public acceptance, environmental protection, product quality, project management, efficiency in operations, governance and reputation.

b) Risk management is an integral part of all organizational processes.
Risk management is not a stand-alone activity that is separate from the main activities and processes of the organization. Risk management is part of the responsibilities of management and an integral part of all organizational processes, including strategic planning and all project and change management processes.

c) Risk management is part of decision making.
Risk management helps decision makers make informed choices, prioritize actions and distinguish among alternative courses of action.

d) Risk management explicitly addresses uncertainty.
Risk management explicitly takes account of uncertainty, the nature of that uncertainty, and how it can be addressed.

e) Risk management is systematic, structured and timely.
A systematic, timely and structured approach to risk management contributes to efficiency and to consistent, comparable and reliable results.

f) Risk management is based on the best available information.
The inputs to the process of managing risk are based on information sources such as historical data, experience, stakeholder feedback, observation, forecasts and expert judgement. However, decision makers should inform themselves of, and should take into account, any limitations of the data or modelling used or the possibility of divergence among experts.

g) Risk management is tailored.
Risk management is aligned with the organization's external and internal context and risk profile.

h) Risk management takes human and cultural factors into account.
Risk management recognizes the capabilities, perceptions and intentions of external and internal people that can facilitate or hinder achievement of the organization's objectives.

i) Risk management is transparent and inclusive.
Appropriate and timely involvement of stakeholders and, in particular, decision makers at all levels of the organization, ensures that risk management remains relevant and up- to- date. Involvement also allows stakeholders to be properly represented and to have their views taken into account in determining risk criteria.

j) Risk management is dynamic, iterative and responsive to change.
Risk management continually senses and responds to change. As external and internal events occur, context and knowledge change, monitoring and review of risks take place, new risks emerge, some change and others disappear.

k) Risk management facilitates continual improvement of the organization.
Organizations should develop and implement strategies to improve their risk management maturity alongside all other aspects of their organization.

(ISO 31000:2009, Clause 3)

3.1.6 Risk management process model

Figure 1 shows the risk management process model as presented in ISO 31000.

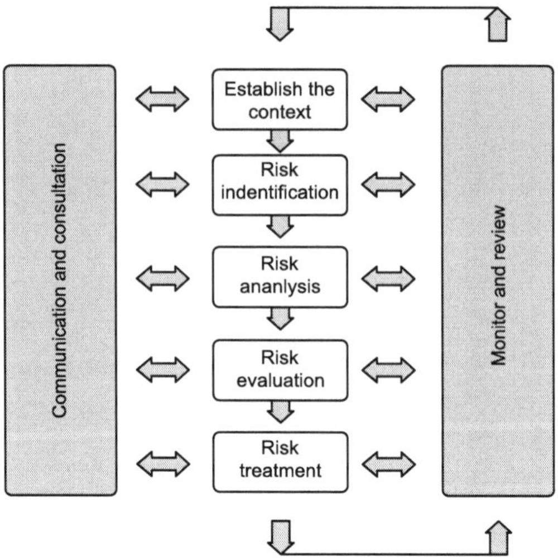

Figure 1 — Risk management process model (based on ISO 31000, Figure 3)

The establishing the context aspect in Figure 1 corresponds to the following clauses from ISO/IEC 27001:

- Understanding the organization and its context (4.1);
- Understanding the needs and expectations of interested parties (4.2).

The risk identification, analysis and evaluation aspects correspond to the risk assessment process described in 6.1.2 of ISO/IEC 27001 and the risk treatment process corresponds to 6.1.3 of ISO/IEC 27001.

The communication aspect corresponds to the communication process described in 7.4 of ISO/IEC 27001. The monitoring and review aspects correspond to the performance evaluation process described in 9 of ISO/IEC 27001.

3.1.7 Delivering effective information security

The ISMS must be able to deliver successful information security if it is to be useful, beneficial and make a positive contribution to the success of the organization. Information security is primarily a management issue, rather than a technical or IT issue. However, one should not ignore the technical problems, especially given the widespread dependence on the use of IT.

Information security management is not a one-off exercise, but should be seen as an ongoing activity of continual improvement adopted by ISO/IEC 27001:2013, as well as other management system standards (MSS) (such as ISO 9001, *Quality management systems — Requirements*). Management support and commitment for the ISMS activities is one of the key factors in achieving a successful and effective ISMS implementation. Well-managed information security should be seen as a business enabler.

3.2 Compatibility with other management system standards (MSS)

The ISO/IEC 27001:2013 edition applies the high-level structure, identical subclause titles, identical text, common terms and core definitions defined in Annex SL of the ISO/IEC Directives, *Part 1 — Consolidated ISO Supplement — Procedures specific to ISO* and therefore maintains compatibility with other MSS that have adopted Annex SL. This common approach defined in Annex SL will be useful for those organizations that choose to operate a single management system that meets the requirements of two or more MSS.

3.3 'Shall' statements

ISO/IEC 27001:2013 takes the form of a set of requirements using prescriptive 'shall' statements, which an organization needs to conform to if compliance is to be claimed. These 'shall' statements are specified in Clauses 4 to 10 of ISO/IEC 27001:2013 and they cover all the requirements associated with the process approach adopted by all MSS.

The term 'shall' indicates those provisions that reflect the requirements of ISO/IEC 27001:2013 that are mandatory. The term 'should' is used to indicate those provisions that, although they constitute guidance for the application of the requirements and are therefore expected to be adopted, are not mandatory.

As a code of practice, ISO/IEC 27002:2013 takes the form of guidance and recommendations, and so contains only 'should' statements and not 'shall' statements. This means ISO/IEC 27002:2013 is not a conformance assessment standard and care needs to be taken to ensure that claims of compliance are not misleading between this standard and ISO/IEC 27001, which is a compliance standard.

4 ISMS requirements

4.1 Context of the organization (Clause 4)

4.1.1 Understanding the organization and its context (4.1)

4.1.1.1 Requirement

'The organization shall determine external and internal issues that are relevant to its purpose and that affect its ability to achieve the intended outcome(s) of its information security management system.'

(ISO/IEC 27001:2013, 4.1)

4.1.1.2 Commentary

Regarding the internal and external context within which an organization will manage risk, the following guidance given in ISO 31000 (5.3) is relevant to ISO/IEC 27001 and information security risks.

> The internal context is the internal environment in which the organization seeks to achieve its objectives.
>
> The risk management process should be aligned with the organization's culture, processes, structure and strategy. Internal context is anything within the organization that can influence the way in which an organization will manage risk. It should be established because:
>
> a) risk management takes place in the context of the objectives of the organization;
> b) objectives and criteria of a particular project, process or activity should be considered in the light of objectives of the organization as a whole; and
> c) some organizations fail to recognize opportunities to achieve their strategic, project or business objectives, and this affects ongoing organizational commitment, credibility, trust and value.

It is necessary to understand the internal context. This can include, but is not limited to:

- governance, organizational structure, roles and accountabilities;
- policies, objectives, and the strategies that are in place to achieve them;
- capabilities, understood in terms of resources and knowledge (e.g. capital, time, people, processes, systems and technologies);
- the relationships with and perceptions and values of internal stakeholders;
- the organization's culture;
- information systems, information flows and decision making processes (both formal and informal);
- standards, guidelines and models adopted by the organization; and
- form and extent of contractual relationships.

(ISO 31000:2009, 5.3.3)

The external context is the external environment in which the organization seeks to achieve its objectives.

Understanding the external context is important in order to ensure that the objectives and concerns of external stakeholders are considered when developing risk criteria. It is based on the organization-wide context, but with specific details of legal and regulatory requirements, stakeholder perceptions and other aspects of risks specific to the scope of the risk management process.

The external context can include, but is not limited to:

- the social and cultural, political, legal, regulatory, financial, technological, economic, natural and competitive environment, whether international, national, regional or local;
- key drivers and trends having impact on the objectives of the organization; and
- relationships with, perceptions and values of external stakeholders.

(ISO 31000:2009, 5.3.2)

4.1.2 Understanding the needs and expectations of interested parties (4.2)

4.1.2.1 Requirements

'The organization shall determine:

a) interested parties that are relevant to the information security management system; and
b) the requirements of these interested parties relevant to information security.'

(ISO/IEC 27001:2013, 4.2)

4.1.2.2 Commentary

The requirements of interested parties relevant to information security can be related to:

- a set of principles, objectives and business requirements for information handling, processing, storing, communicating and archiving that an organization has developed to support its operations, business applications and services;
- legal, statutory, regulatory or contractual obligations that an organization, its trading partners, contractors and service providers have to satisfy, and their socio-cultural environment;
- the information security risk management process – assessing and treating the risks to the organization, taking into account the organization's overall business strategy and objectives.

ISO/IEC 27002:2013 provides guidance on different aspects of information security requirements including:

- Mobile devices and teleworking (6.2);
- Information classification (8.2);
- Business requirements of access control (9.1);
- System and application access control (9.4);
- Physical and environmental security (Clause 11);
- Backups (12.3);
- Network security management (13.1);
- Information transfer (13.2);
- Confidentiality or non-disclosure agreements (13.2.4);
- Information security in supplier relationships (15.1);
- Information security aspects of business continuity management (Clause 17);
- Compliance with legal and contractual requirements (18.1).

4.1.3 Determining the scope of the information security management system (4.3)

4.1.3.1 Requirements

The organization shall determine the boundaries and applicability of the information security management system to establish its scope.

When determining this scope, the organization shall consider:

a) the external and internal issues referred to in 4.1;
b) the requirements referred to in 4.2; and
c) interfaces and dependencies between activities performed by the organization, and those that are performed by other organizations.

(ISO/IEC 27001:2013, 4.3)

4.1.3.2 Commentary

The scope of the ISMS may be limited to part(s) of the organization or the scope may be defined to be the whole organization. Whatever the size and nature of the ISMS scope, its definition must address the internal and external context (4.1) and the needs, expectations and requirements of interested parties (4.2). It is entirely up to the organization to choose the scope of the ISMS that is appropriate, but, in any case, the boundaries associated with the ISMS scope need to be well-defined and complete. This means the scope needs to take account of the interfaces and dependencies, with internal and external activities, and its applicability to other parts of the organization (not within the ISMS scope), other organizations, third-party suppliers, or any other entity outside the ISMS. Details of any exclusions from the scope of the ISMS shall be documented and properly justified. When excluding parts of the business from the ISMS scope, take care that any information exchange with the excluded part of the organization is identified and addressed using the interfaces and dependencies described above. See also 5.3.3.2.4, 'ISMS scope', of this guide.

4.2 Leadership (Clause 5)

4.2.1 Leadership and commitment (5.1)

4.2.1.1 Requirements

Top management shall demonstrate leadership and commitment with respect to the information security management system by:

a) ensuring the information security policy and the information security objectives are established and are compatible with the strategic direction of the organization;
b) ensuring the integration of the information security management system
requirements into the organization's processes;
c) ensuring that the resources needed for the information security management system are available;
d) communicating the importance of effective information security management and of conforming to the information security management system requirements;
e) ensuring that the information security management system achieves its intended outcome(s);
f) directing and supporting persons to contribute to the effectiveness of the information security management system;
g) promoting continual improvement; and
h) supporting other relevant management roles to demonstrate their leadership as it applies to their areas of responsibility.

(ISO/IEC 27001:2013, 5.1)

4.2.1.2 Commentary

It is important that management shall demonstrate its commitment and proactive leadership for the processes and activities that are involved in the establishment, implementation, operation, monitoring and review, maintenance and improvement of the ISMS in accordance with the requirements of ISO/IEC 27001:2013. This commitment shall include from establishing information security policy, setting objectives, allocating roles and responsibilities, communicating the importance of information security management to the business, provisioning resources for the ISMS and deciding upon the risk acceptance criteria and acceptable level of risk through to conducting management reviews. Management commitment needs to be real, positive, visible and accountable support. Decisions made by management need to be documented, and these documented decisions can be used to provide evidence of the involvement management has in the information security management process.

The organization shall ensure that it provides adequate resources to implement the requirements and processes identified in the ISMS standard; this includes all that is defined in Clauses 4 to 10. It shall also ensure that these resources are managed appropriately according to ISO/IEC 27001:2013, 5.2. There are several activities where resources are needed (see 4.4.1): the resources to conduct the risk assessment, the resources needed for the implementation of controls, the resources needed for the training, and the resources necessary to keep the once-established ISMS up to date and effective in day-to-day business. For each of these activities, plans should be in place that support the allocation of sufficient resources.

4.2.2 Policy (5.2)

4.2.2.1 Requirements

Top management shall establish an information security policy that:

a) is appropriate to the purpose of the organization;
b) includes information security objectives (see 6.2) or provides the framework for setting information security objectives;
c) includes a commitment to satisfy applicable requirements related to information security; and
d) includes a commitment to continual improvement of the information security management system.

The information security policy shall:

e) be available as documented information;
f) be communicated within the organization; and
g) be available to interested parties, as appropriate.

(ISO/IEC 27001:2013, 5.2)

4.2.2.2 Commentary

An 'information security policy' is established for the organization and approved by its top management. This policy sets out the organization's approach to managing its information security objectives. This information security policy should, for example, address requirements created by:

- business strategy and objectives, taking account of the business context (see 4.1.1) and business requirements from interested parties (see 4.1.2);
- regulations, legislation and contracts;
- the current and projected information security risk and threat environment.

The high-level top management information security policy should be supported by topic-specific policies, which further mandate the implementation of information security controls and are typically structured to address the needs of certain target groups within an organization or to cover certain topics. ISO/IEC 27002:2013 defines the following as examples of such detailed policy topics (clause references relate to ISO/IEC 27002:2013):

- Access control (Clause 9);
- Information classification (and handling) (8.2);
- Physical and environmental security (Clause 11);
- End user-oriented topics such as:
  - Acceptable use of assets (8.1.3);
  - Clear desk and clear screen policy (11.2.9);
  - Information transfer (13.2.1);
  - Mobile devices and teleworking (6.2);
  - Restrictions on software installation and use (12.6.2);
- Backup (12.3);
- Protection from malware (12.2);
- Management of technical vulnerabilities (12.6.1);
- Cryptographic controls (10.1);
- Communications security (Clause 13);
- Privacy and protection of personally identifiable information (18.1.4);
- Supplier relationships (Clause 15).

The need for internal policies for information security and the level of detail and content of such policies varies across organizations, depending on their size, complexity and nature of their business. Policies for information security can be issued in a single 'information security policy' document or as a set of individual but related documents.

If any of the organization's information security policies are distributed outside the organization, care should be taken not to disclose confidential information.

4.2.3 Organizational roles, responsibilities and authorities (5.3)

4.2.3.1 Requirements

> Top management shall ensure that the responsibilities and authorities for roles relevant to information security are assigned and communicated.
>
> Top management shall assign the responsibility and authority for:
>
> a) ensuring that the information security management system conforms to the requirements of this International Standard; and
> b) reporting on the performance of the information security management system to top management.
>
> (ISO/IEC 27001:2013, 5.3)

4.2.3.2 Commentary

Allocation of information security responsibilities should be done in accordance with the organization's information security policies. Management should require all employees and contractors to apply information security in accordance with the established policies and procedures of the organization.

ISO/IEC 27002:2013 cites the following management responsibilities as best practice for

> ...ensuring that employees and contractors:
>
> a) are properly briefed on their information security roles and responsibilities prior to being granted access to confidential information or information systems;
> b) are provided with guidelines to state information security expectations of their role within the organization;
> c) are motivated to fulfil the information security policies of the organization;
> d) achieve a level of awareness on information security relevant to their roles and responsibilities within the organization (see 7.2.2);
> e) conform to the terms and conditions of employment, which includes the organization's information security policy and appropriate methods of working;
> f) continue to have the appropriate skills and qualifications and are educated on a regular basis;
> g) are provided with an anonymous reporting channel to report violations of information security policies or procedures ("whistle blowing").
>
> (ISO/IEC 27002:2013, 7.2.1)

Responsibilities for the protection of individual assets and for carrying out specific information security processes should be identified and assigned. Responsibilities for information security risk management activities and, in particular, for acceptance of residual risks should be defined.

If individuals with allocated information security responsibilities delegate security tasks to others it should be understood that the individual still remains accountable and should determine that any delegated tasks have been correctly performed.

4.3 Planning (Clause 6)

4.3.1 Actions to address risks and opportunities (6.1)

4.3.1.1 Requirements

4.3.1.1.1 General

When planning for the information security management system, the organization shall consider the issues referred to in 4.1 and the requirements referred to in 4.2 and determine the risks and opportunities that need to be addressed to:

a) ensure the information security management system can achieve its intended outcome(s);
b) prevent, or reduce, undesired effects; and
c) achieve continual improvement.

The organization shall plan:

d) actions to address these risks and opportunities; and
e) how to
   1) integrate and implement these actions into its information security management system processes; and
   2) evaluate the effectiveness of these actions.

(ISO/IEC 27001:2013, 6.1.1)

4.3.1.1.2 Information security risk assessment

The organization shall define and apply an information security risk assessment process that:

a) establishes and maintains information security risk criteria that include:
   1) the risk acceptance criteria; and
   2) criteria for performing information security risk assessments;
b) ensures that repeated information security risk assessments produce consistent, valid and comparable results;
c) identifies the information security risks:
   1) apply the information security risk assessment process to identify risks associated with the loss of confidentiality, integrity and availability for information within the scope of the information security management system; and
   2) identify the risk owners;
d) analyses the information security risks:
   1) assess the potential consequences that would result if the risks identified in 6.1.2 c) 1) were to materialize;

2) assess the realistic likelihood of the occurrence of the risks identified in 6.1.2 c) 1); and
3) determine the levels of risk;

e) evaluates the information security risks:
1) compare the results of risk analysis with the risk criteria established in 6.1.2 a); and
2) prioritize the analysed risks for risk treatment.

(ISO/IEC 27001:2013, 6.1.2)

4.3.1.1.3 Information security risk treatment

The organization shall define and apply an information security risk treatment process to:

a) select appropriate information security risk treatment options, taking account of the risk assessment results;
b) determine all controls that are necessary to implement the information security risk treatment option(s) chosen;
c) compare the controls determined in 6.1.3 b) above with those in Annex A and verify that no necessary controls have been omitted;...
d) produce a Statement of Applicability that contains the necessary controls (see 6.1.3 b) and c)) and justification for inclusions, whether they are implemented or not, and the justification for exclusions of controls from Annex A;
e) formulate an information security risk treatment plan; and
f) obtain risk owners' approval of the information security risk treatment plan and acceptance of the residual information security risks.

(ISO/IEC 27001:2013, 6.1.3)

4.3.1.2 Commentary

4.3.1.2.1 General (6.1.1)

The organization needs to decide upon actions to address the risks and opportunities. This includes a plan for the actions to be taken as a result of the risk assessment (6.1.2 and, subsequently, 8.2) and actions for risk treatment (6.1.3 and, subsequently, 8.3), as well as actions that identify opportunities for improvement of processes and systems, and how to maximize these opportunities (ISO 31000). The organization also needs to plan how to integrate and implement these actions into its ISMS processes (8.1), and evaluate the effectiveness of these actions (9.1).

4.3.1.2.2 Information security risk assessment (6.1.2)

The organization needs to include its criteria for accepting risks and the identification of acceptable levels of risk.

There are various standards and guidelines that provide help with information security risk management. These include ISO 31000, IEC/ISO 31010, ISO/IEC 27005, BS 7799-3 and BIP 076. The requirements for risk management defined in ISO/IEC 27001 allow a flexible approach to what risk assessment methods can be used by the organization. It is important to note that whatever method is used, it needs to deal with management system requirements in ISO/IEC 27001, including all the control areas of Annex A. The risk method adopted needs to cover the risks related to organizational aspects, personnel controls, business processes, operational, communications and maintenance processes, physical security and procedures, legal, regulatory and contractual matters, and information-processing facilities. In addition, the risk assessment methodology employed should ensure that risk assessments produce comparable and reproducible results; this is especially important when evaluating the risk situation over time. The method of risk assessment that an organization adopts is entirely the decision of the organization.

Risk assessment is a mandatory requirement in ISO/IEC 27001:2013, but this does not require the use of any specific technology or software tools, even though in many situations there are benefits in the use of such tools. This is especially the case when risks need to be re-assessed and risk-related information, such as threats, vulnerabilities and assets, needs to be updated. The complexity of the risk assessment method and approach will depend on the complexity of the ISMS under review. The techniques employed should be consistent with the complexity and the levels of assurance required by the organization. It is important to ensure that all information assets within the ISMS are identified, as these are the basis of the risk assessment, and that an owner is identified and documented for each of the assets. The identification of impacts that the losses of confidentiality, integrity and availability may have on the information assets should take account of the identified legal, regulatory, contractual and business requirements that might be endangered through such losses.

When assessing the likelihood of occurrence of incidents, it is useful to look at documented information and reports of internal incidents that have happened in the past, and to take account of reports, statistics, news and trends obtained from research. Based on these results, the organization needs to estimate the level of risk and to determine whether the risks are acceptable or require treatment, using the risk acceptance criteria established, and taking account of the business context.

The following guidance from ISO 31000 (5.3.5) regarding defining the risk criteria is relevant to ISO/IEC 27001:2013 and information security risks.

The organization should define criteria to be used to evaluate the significance of risk. The criteria should reflect the organization's values, objectives and resources. Some criteria can be imposed by, or derived from, legal and regulatory requirements and other requirements to which the organization subscribes. Risk criteria should be consistent with the organization's risk management policy (see 4.3.2), be defined at the beginning of any risk management process and be continually reviewed.

When defining risk criteria, factors to be considered should include the following:

- the nature and types of causes and consequences that can occur and how they will be measured;
- how likelihood will be defined;
- the timeframe(s) of the likelihood and/or consequence(s);
- how the level of risk is to be determined;
- the views of stakeholders;
- the level at which risk becomes acceptable or tolerable; and
- whether combinations of multiple risks should be taken into account and, if so, how and which combinations should be considered.

(ISO 31000:2009, 5.3.5)

4.3.1.2.2.1 Identification of risks

The following guidance is based on that given in ISO 31000 and IEC/ISO 31010, and is applicable to ISO/IEC 27001 and information security risks.

Risk identification is the process of finding, recognizing and recording risks. The purpose of risk identification is to identify what might happen or what situations might exist that might affect the achievement of the objectives of the system or organization.

(IEC/ISO 31010:2009, 5.2)

The organization should identify sources of risk, areas of impacts, events (including changes in circumstances) and their causes and their potential consequences. The aim of this step is to generate a comprehensive list of risks based on those events that might create, enhance, prevent, degrade, accelerate or delay the achievement of objectives. It is important to identify the risks associated with not pursuing an opportunity. Comprehensive identification is critical, because a risk that is not identified at this stage will not be included in further analysis.

> Identification should include risks whether or not their source is under the control of the organization, even though the risk source or cause may not be evident. Risk identification should include examination of the knock-on effects of particular consequences, including cascade and cumulative effects. It should also consider a wide range of consequences even if the risk source or cause may not be evident. As well as identifying what might happen, it is necessary to consider possible causes and scenarios that show what consequences can occur. All significant causes and consequences should be considered.
>
> The organization should apply risk identification tools and techniques that are suited to its objectives and capabilities, and to the risks faced. Relevant and up-to-date information is important in identifying risks. This should include appropriate background information where possible. People with appropriate knowledge should be involved in identifying risks.
>
> (ISO 31000:2009, 5.4.2)

With specific regard to an organization's ISMS, the risk identification needs to be done in the context of the loss of confidentiality, integrity and availability with regard to the organization's information assets.

It is important that 'The organization should ensure that there is accountability, authority and appropriate competence for managing [ISMS] risk...' (ISO 31000, 4.3.3). Also it is necessary to identify risk owners who have the accountability and authority to manage risks.

4.3.1.2.2.2 Analyses of risks

The following guidance is based on that given in IEC/ISO 31010, and is applicable to ISO/IEC 27001 and information security risks.

> Risk analysis is about developing an understanding of the risk. It provides an input to risk assessment and to decisions about whether risks need to be treated and about the most appropriate treatment strategies and methods.
>
> Risk analysis consists of determining the consequences and their probabilities for identified risk events, taking into account the presence (or not) and the effectiveness of any existing controls. The consequences and their probabilities are then combined to determine a level of risk.

Risk analysis involves consideration of the causes and sources of risk, their consequences and the probability that those consequences can occur. Factors that affect consequences and probability should be identified. An event can have multiple consequences and can affect multiple objectives. Existing risk controls and their effectiveness should be taken into account....

Risk analysis normally includes an estimation of the range of potential consequences that might arise from an event, situation or circumstance, and their associated probabilities, in order to measure the level of risk. However in some instances, such as where the consequences are likely to be insignificant, or the probability is expected to be extremely low, a single parameter estimate may be sufficient for a decision to be made[.]

In some circumstances, a consequence can occur as a result of a range of different events or conditions, or where the specific event is not identified. In this case, the focus of risk assessment is on analysing the importance and vulnerability of components of the system with a view to defining treatments which relate to levels of protection or recovery strategies.

Methods used in analysing risks can be qualitative, semi-quantitative or quantitative. The degree of detail required will depend upon the particular application, the availability of reliable data and the decision-making needs of the organization. Some methods and the degree of detail of the analysis may be prescribed by legislation.

Qualitative assessment defines consequence, probability and level of risk by significance levels such as "high", "medium" and "low", may combine consequence and probability, and evaluates the resultant level of risk against qualitative criteria.

Semi-quantitative methods use numerical rating scales for consequence and probability and combine them to produce a level of risk using a formula. Scales may be linear or logarithmic, or have some other relationship; formulae used can also vary.

Quantitative analysis estimates practical values for consequences and their probabilities, and produces values of the level of risk in specific units defined when developing the context. Full quantitative analysis may not always be possible or desirable due to insufficient information about the system or activity being analysed, lack of data, influence of human factors, etc. or because the effort of quantitative analysis is not warranted or required. In such circumstances, a comparative semi-quantitative or qualitative ranking of risks by specialists, knowledgeable in their respective field, may still be effective.

In cases where the analysis is qualitative, there should be a clear explanation of all the terms employed and the basis for all criteria should be recorded.

Even where full quantification has been carried out, it needs to be recognized that the levels of risk calculated are estimates. Care should be taken to ensure that they are not attributed a level of accuracy and precision inconsistent with the accuracy of the data and methods employed.

Levels of risk should be expressed in the most suitable terms for that type of risk and in a form that aids risk evaluation. In some instances, the magnitude of a risk can be expressed as a probability distribution over a range of consequences.

(IEC/ISO 31010:2009, 5.3.1)

NOTE (on terminology)

Likelihood
chance of something happening
NOTE 1 In risk management terminology, the word "likelihood" is used to refer to the chance of something happening, whether defined, measured or determined objectively or subjectively, qualitatively or quantitatively, and described using general terms or mathematically [such as a **probability** (3.6.1.4) or a **frequency** (3.6.1.5) over a given time period].

NOTE 2 The English term "likelihood" does not have a direct equivalent in some languages; instead, the equivalent of the term "probability" is often used. However, in English, "probability" is often narrowly interpreted as a mathematical term. Therefore, in risk management terminology, "likelihood" is used with the intent that it should have the same broad interpretation as the term "probability" has in many languages other than English.

(ISO Guide 73:2009, 3.6.1.1)

4.3.1.2.2.3 Evaluation of risks

The following guidance is based on that given in ISO 31000 and IEC/ISO 31010, and is applicable to ISO/IEC 27001 and information security risks.

The purpose of risk evaluation is to assist in making decisions, based on the outcomes of risk analysis, about which risks need treatment and the priority for treatment implementation.

> Risk evaluation involves comparing estimated levels of risk with risk criteria defined when the context was established, in order to determine the significance of the level and type of risk.
>
> Risk evaluation uses the understanding of risk obtained during risk analysis to make decisions about future actions. Ethical, legal, financial and other considerations, including perceptions of risk, are also inputs to the decision....
>
> The nature of the decisions that need to be made and the criteria which will be used to make those decisions were decided when establishing the context but they need to be revisited in more detail at this stage now that more is known about the particular risks identified....
>
> The decision about whether and how to treat the risk may depend on the costs and benefits of taking the risk and the costs and benefits of implementing improved controls.
>
> (IEC/ISO 31010:2009, 5.4)

4.3.1.2.3 Information security risk treatment (6.1.3)

Once the organization has identified, assessed and understood the impact the risks might have on its business, it can take various actions to manage and treat these risks appropriately within its business context. The following guidance is based on that given in ISO 31000 and is applicable to ISO/IEC 27001 and information security risks.

> Risk treatment involves a cyclical process of:
>
> - assessing a risk treatment;
> - deciding whether residual risk levels are tolerable;
> - if not tolerable, generating a new risk treatment; and
> - assessing the effectiveness of that treatment.
>
> Risk treatment options are not necessarily mutually exclusive or appropriate in all circumstances. The options can include the following:
>
> a) avoiding the risk by deciding not to start or continue with the activity that gives rise to the risk;
> b) taking or increasing the risk in order to pursue an opportunity;
> c) removing the risk source;
> d) changing the likelihood;
> e) changing the consequences;
> f) sharing the risk with another party or parties (including contracts and risk financing); and
> g) retaining the risk by informed decision.

> (ISO 31000:2009, 5.5.1)

Which of these options, or other options, or a combination of several of these options, the organization takes is entirely up to the organization – different organizations might come to different conclusions for the same risk, depending on business objectives and circumstances. In any case, it is important for an ISMS certification audit that these decisions are well-documented, and that the organization can provide evidence that these decisions have been taken in full knowledge of the risks, and not simply through ignorance.

> Selecting the most appropriate risk treatment option involves balancing the costs and efforts of implementation against the benefits derived, with regard to legal, regulatory, and other requirements such as social responsibility and the protection of the natural environment. Decisions should also take into account risks which can warrant risk treatment that is not justifiable on economic grounds, e.g. severe (high negative consequence) but rare (low likelihood) risks.
>
> (ISO 31000:2009, 5.5.2)

If the organization decides to apply controls to manage and treat the risk then it first needs to select a system of controls that are suitable for this purpose. The identification of controls (6.1.3 b)) should take account of the risk acceptance criteria (6.1.2 a)1)), how much the controls reduce the risks, and the identified legal, regulatory and contractual requirements.

The organization needs to 'determine all controls that are necessary to implement the information security risk treatment option(s)...' that are selected (6.1.3 b)). Organizations can design security controls as required to meet their specific requirements, or identify them from any source. The organization needs to 'compare the controls...' it has determined to be necessary '...with those in Annex A and verify that no necessary controls have been omitted;...Annex A contains a comprehensive list of control objectives and controls. Users...are directed to Annex A to ensure that no necessary controls are overlooked....Control objectives are implicitly included in the controls chosen. The control objectives and controls listed in Annex A are not exhaustive and additional control objectives and controls may be needed' (6.1.3 c)). The organization needs to 'produce a Statement of Applicability that contains the necessary controls (see 6.1.3 b) and c)) and justification for inclusions, whether they are implemented or not, and the justification for exclusions of controls from Annex A' (6.1.3 d)).

The identification of controls should be cost-effective, i.e. the cost of their implementation should not exceed the financial impact of the risks they are intended to reduce. Of course, some impacts will be non-financial. Account should also be taken of those impacts related to safety, personal information, legal and regulatory obligations, image and reputation. In addition, the residual risks that remain after the controls have been implemented need to be assessed. These residual risks are generally difficult to assess, but at least an estimate should be made of how much the controls address the identified security requirements, to obtain an indication whether more controls are necessary.

The risk treatment plan shall outline what management actions need to be taken to manage the identified risks, the priority of these actions, limiting factors, deadlines and the necessary resources. The responsibilities of those involved in the process of managing the information security risks need to be clearly allocated, as well as the relevant information security responsibilities of users and managers in the ISMS. Other business processes and their schedules might need to be coordinated with the risk treatment plan.

The organization shall have a set of processes in place for implementation of the risk treatment plan and the system of selected control objectives and controls, taking account of the funding for the ISMS and the allocation of roles and responsibilities. The identified actions, roles and responsibilities involved in this process should be documented.

4.3.2 Information security objectives and plans to achieve them (6.2)

4.3.2.1 Requirements

The organization shall establish information security objectives at relevant functions and levels.

The information security objectives shall:

a) be consistent with the information security policy;
b) be measurable (if practicable);
c) take into account applicable information security requirements, and risk assessment and risk treatment results;
d) be communicated; and
e) be updated as appropriate.

The organization shall retain documented information on the information security objectives.

When planning how to achieve its information security objectives, the organization shall determine:

f) what will be done;
g) what resources will be required;

h) who will be responsible;
i) when it will be completed; and
j) how the results will be evaluated.

(ISO/IEC 27001:2013, 6.2)

4.3.2.2 Commentary

There are a number of things to be considered when formulating a set of information security objectives. As a minimum the organization needs to consider:

- its own business information, its clients' and customers' information that it processes and any personally identifiable information that it handles, with respect to safeguarding the confidentiality, integrity and availability of this information;
- protection of its business resources from fraud, theft, abuse, misuse and any form of damage;
- ensuring there is appropriate responsibility and accountability for information security established throughout the business;
- ensuring employees and staff have an appropriate level of awareness, knowledge and skill to allow them to maintain an effective level of information security and to minimize the effects and impacts of information security incidents, threats and attacks;
- continuity and availability of its commercial activities in the event of significant information security incidents, system failures, denial of service attacks and major disruption of business.

Plans to implement the organization's information security objectives need to be in place, these plans need to be communicated to those that need to implement these plans, and the plans need to be reviewed and updated accordingly to ensure they are still relevant to the organization. The results of implementing these plans need to be reviewed and evaluated to check whether they provide effective and sufficient protection of the organization's information assets.

4.4 Support (Clause 7)

4.4.1 Resources (7.1)

4.4.1.1 Requirement

'The organization shall determine and provide the resources needed for the establishment, implementation, maintenance and continual improvement of the information security management system.'

(ISO/IEC 27001:2013, 7.1)

4.4.1.2 Commentary

The organization needs to allocate appropriate management and technical resources to deal with the ISMS processes, that is, in terms of capital, time, people, processes, systems, technologies, and training and awareness programmes. Human resources are needed with the necessary skills, experience and competence to deal with each step in establishing, implementing, maintaining and continually improving the ISMS.

Depending on the size and complexity of the organization the amount of resource will vary. As regards human resources, the overall management of the ISMS might be charged to a security department or to a security team, consisting of a number of individuals, or a single individual. Other related ISMS tasks might be charged to other individuals throughout the organization and even support from external contracted services might be deployed. If work is delegated under contract to external parties, the organization must ensure that there is appropriate accountability, authority and competence for managing the ISMS and the associated risks, for example, identifying risk owners who have the accountability and authority to manage the ISMS risks, and identifying who is accountable for the development, implementation and maintenance of the ISMS.

4.4.2 Competence (7.2)

4.4.2.1 Requirements

The organization shall:

a) determine the necessary competence of person(s) doing work under its control that affects its information security performance;
b) ensure that these persons are competent on the basis of appropriate education, training, or experience;
c) where applicable, take actions to acquire the necessary competence, and evaluate the effectiveness of the actions taken; and
d) retain appropriate documented information as evidence of competence.

(ISO/IEC 27001:2013, 7.2)

4.4.2.2 Commentary

The type and range of competence regarding knowledge and skill of information security will depend on the specific job function. Those directly involved in the establishment and implementation of the organization's ISMS should, as a minimum, have experience, knowledge and specific training regarding:

- ISO/IEC 27001:2013 and other relevant normative documents;
- information security concepts and techniques, policies and procedures;
- risk assessment and risk treatment methods, and an understanding of risk management from the business perspective;
- an understanding of the ISMS controls and their implementation, defined in ISO/IEC 27002:2013, and any other controls the organization needs to implement;
- incident-handling methods and business continuity;
- performance evaluation (ISO/IEC 27001:2013, 9.1);
- current technology where information security might be relevant or an issue.

4.4.3 Awareness (7.3)

4.4.3.1 Requirements

> Persons doing work under the organization's control shall be aware of:
>
> a) the information security policy;
> b) their contribution to the effectiveness of the information security management system, including the benefits of improved information security performance; and
> c) the implications of not conforming with the information security management system requirements.
>
> (ISO/IEC 27001:2013, 7.3)

4.4.3.2 Commentary

It is best practice to implement a training and awareness programme. The organization should roll out an appropriate awareness and training programme, ensuring that all personnel with assigned ISMS responsibilities are competent to perform their tasks. The programme shall determine the necessary competencies, provide training to satisfy these requirements, evaluate the effectiveness of the training and maintain records of the skills and qualifications achieved.

It is also important to remember that security is not there to prevent staff from doing what they are employed to do – training should enable them to do their job with managed and effective security control. It should enable them to demonstrate their fulfilled accountabilities, establish their trustworthiness without leaving a trail of doubts, and improve their qualifications. Staff will soon see well-implemented security as a benefit, rather than as an inconvenience.

The organization shall identify the requirements for training and awareness, and ensure that it provides appropriate training to all users, staff and managers to ensure that the ISMS is effective and that information security is marketed as an important day-to-day aspect of business. The training given should be commensurate with the job role and function, and the specific responsibilities for information security. As part of its general training and awareness programme, the organization should include information security management. It needs to ensure it has allocated the right roles and responsibilities to those that have been trained, and that these individuals are competent in dealing with information security management issues. These can range from a simple level of understanding and competence that all staff should have, e.g. handling passwords, the basics of physical security, the proper use of email, and virus protection, through to more involved levels that not all staff would be expected to be competent in, e.g. configuring a firewall and managing the information security incident-handling process.

Documented information related to the training that employees of the organization have attended should be maintained to provide an overview of the skill set of the personnel and to provide evidence of the training activities implemented by the organization. It is also necessary to evaluate how effective the training was and whether the intended objectives were achieved.

The following guidance from ISO/IEC 27002:2013 is applicable to awareness on matters concerning information security.

> An information security awareness programme should aim to make employees and, where relevant, contractors aware of their responsibilities for information security and the means by which those responsibilities are discharged.
>
> An information security awareness programme should be established in line with the organization's information security policies and relevant procedures, taking into consideration the organization's information to be protected and the controls that have been implemented to protect the information. The awareness programme should include a number of awareness-raising activities such as campaigns (e.g. an "information security day") and issuing booklets or newsletters.

The awareness programme should be planned taking into consideration the employees' roles in the organization, and, where relevant, the organization's expectation of the awareness of contractors. The activities in the awareness programme should be scheduled over time, preferably regularly, so that the activities are repeated and cover new employees and contractors. The awareness programme should also be updated regularly so it stays in line with organizational policies and procedures, and should be built on lessons learnt from information security incidents.

Awareness training should be performed as required by the organization's information security awareness programme. Awareness training can use different delivery media including classroom-based, distance learning, web-based, self-paced and others.

Information security education and training should also cover general aspects such as:

a) stating management's commitment to information security throughout the organization;
b) the need to become familiar with and comply with applicable information security rules and obligations, as defined in policies, standards, laws, regulations, contracts and agreements;
c) personal accountability for one's own actions and inactions, and general responsibilities towards securing or protecting information belonging to the organization and external parties;
d) basic information security procedures (such as information security incident reporting) and baseline controls (such as password security, malware controls and clear desks);
e) contact points and resources for additional information and advice on information security matters, including further information security education and training materials.

Information security education and training should take place periodically. Initial education and training applies to those who transfer to new positions or roles with substantially different information security requirements, not just to new starters and should take place before the role becomes active.

The organization should develop the education and training programme in order to conduct the education and training effectively. The programme should be in line with the organization's information security policies and relevant procedures, taking into consideration the organization's information to be protected and the controls that have been implemented to protect the information. The programme should consider different forms of education and training, e.g. lectures or self-studies.

(ISO/IEC 27002:2013, 7.2.2)

4.4.4 Communication (7.4)

4.4.4.1 Requirements

> The organization shall determine the need for internal and external communications relevant to the information security management system including:
>
> a) on what to communicate;
> b) when to communicate;
> c) with whom to communicate;
> d) who shall communicate; and
> e) the processes by which communication shall be effected.
>
> (ISO/IEC 27001:2013, 7.4)

4.4.4.2 Commentary

There are many aspects of information security where it is essential that effective communication channels are in place, for example, with regard to reporting information security events, incidents and weaknesses.

> All employees and contractors should be made aware of their responsibility to report information security events as quickly as possible. They should also be aware of the procedure for reporting information security events and the point of contact to which the events should be reported.
>
> (ISO/IEC 27002:2013, 16.1.2)
>
> Employees and contractors using the organization's information systems and services should be required to note and report any observed or suspected information security weaknesses in systems or services.
>
> (ISO/IEC 27002:2013, 16.1.3)

In both these cases individuals will need to know with whom to communicate, and how to communicate the information.

ISO 31000 gives the following general guidance regarding the risk management process, which is relevant and applicable to the establishment, implementation and maintenance of the ISMS as per the requirements of ISO/IEC 27001:

> Communication and consultation with external and internal stakeholders should take place during all stages of the risk management process.

> Therefore, plans for communication and consultation should be developed at an early stage. These should address issues relating to the risk itself, its causes, its consequences (if known), and the measures being taken to treat it. Effective external and internal communication and consultation should take place to ensure that those accountable for implementing the risk management process and stakeholders understand the basis on which decisions are made, and the reasons why particular actions are required....
>
> Communication and consultation with stakeholders is important as they make judgements about risk based on their perceptions of risk. These perceptions can vary due to differences in values, needs, assumptions, concepts and concerns of stakeholders. As their views can have a significant impact on the decisions made, the stakeholders' perceptions should be identified, recorded, and taken into account in the decision making process.
>
> (ISO 31000:2009, 5.2)

Other examples include communications relating to:

- information security policies – 'A set of policies for information security should be defined, approved by management, published and communicated to employees and relevant external parties' (ISO/IEC 27002:2013, 5.1.1);
- contact with authorities – 'Appropriate contacts with relevant authorities should be maintained....Organizations should have procedures in place that specify when and by whom authorities (e.g. law enforcement, regulatory bodies, supervisory authorities) should be contacted and how identified information security incidents should be reported in a timely manner (e.g. if it is suspected that laws may have been broken)' (ISO/IEC 27002:2013, 6.1.3);
- confidentiality or non-disclosure agreements – 'h) process for notification and reporting of unauthorized disclosure or confidential information leakage' (ISO/IEC 27002:2013, 13.2.4);
- information security in supplier relationships (ISO/IEC 27002:2013, 15.1);
- monitoring and review of supplier services (ISO/IEC 27002:2013, 15.2.1);
- business continuity – communications within and without the organization.

4.4.5 Documented information (7.5)

4.4.5.1 Requirements

4.4.5.1.1 General

The organization's information security management system shall include:

a) documented information required by this International Standard; and
b) documented information determined by the organization as being necessary for the effectiveness of the information security management system.

(ISO/IEC 27001:2013, 7.5.1)

4.4.5.1.2 Creating and updating

When creating and updating documented information the organization shall ensure appropriate:

a) identification and description (e.g. a title, date, author, or reference number);
b) format (e.g. language, software version, graphics) and media (e.g. paper, electronic); and
c) review and approval for suitability and adequacy.

(ISO/IEC 27001:2013, 7.5.2)

4.4.5.1.3 Control of documented information

Documented information required by the information security management system and by this International Standard shall be controlled to ensure:

a) it is available and suitable for use, where and when it is needed; and
b) it is adequately protected (e.g. from loss of confidentiality, improper use, or loss of integrity).

For the control of documented information, the organization shall address the following activities, as applicable:

c) distribution, access, retrieval and use;
d) storage and preservation, including the preservation of legibility;
e) control of changes (e.g. version control); and
f) retention and disposition.

> Documented information of external origin, determined by the organization to be necessary for the planning and operation of the information security management system, shall be identified as appropriate, and controlled.
>
> (ISO/IEC 27001:2013, 7.5.3)

4.4.5.2 Commentary

The extent of documented information for an ISMS can differ from one organization to another due to:

- the size of organization and its type of activities, processes, products and services;
- the complexity of processes and their interactions; and
- the competence of persons.

4.4.5.2.1 System of documented information

The mandatory set of documented information required by ISO/IEC 27001:2013 includes information regarding:

- the scope of the ISMS (4.3);
- the information security policy (5.2);
- the information security risk assessment process (6.1.2);
- the information security risk treatment process (6.1.3);
- the information security objectives (6.2);
- '...results of the information security risk assessments' (8.2);
- '...results of the information security risk treatment' (8.3) – including a Statement of Applicability (see 6.1.3);
- '...the monitoring and measurement results' (9.1);
- '...the audit programme(s) and the audit results' (9.2);
- '...the results of management reviews' (9.3);
- '...the nature of the nonconformities and any subsequent actions taken...' (10.1);
- '...the results of any corrective action' (10.1).

The control requirements for documented information in ISO/IEC 27001:2013 are harmonized with the requirements specified in other MSS, e.g. ISO 9001 and ISO/IEC 20000-1. This offers several benefits to an organization, including the opportunity to have combined/integrated audits, and economize on the resources needed to manage and maintain the system of documentation and records, providing better control of the business assets and smoother, more integrated management.

4.4.5.2.2 Control and protection

It is important that documented information of the ISMS is properly controlled and adequately protected. This means the organization needs to have an appropriate set of controls, procedures and processes in place to ensure such information is adequately protected and controlled to meet the organization's requirements for the integrity, availability and confidentiality of such documented information. This is an important part of the risk management process alongside the other controls for information security. All documented information that is necessary to operate the ISMS and to provide evidence that the ISMS is performing and operating correctly and efficiently should be maintained, should be current and should be relevant. It is also important that the documented information contains sufficient detail to provide evidence of the correct and effective functioning of the ISMS. For example, the documented information covers the results of the risk assessment and actions pertaining to the decisions regarding risk treatments. Another example might be management meetings and decisions, and details of actions that have been taken and are traceable to these management decisions and/or to the policies and standards that the organization is applying.

4.5 Operation (Clause 8)

4.5.1 Operational planning and control (8.1)

4.5.1.1 Requirements

> The organization shall plan, implement and control the processes needed to meet information security requirements, and to implement the actions determined in 6.1. The organization shall also implement plans to achieve information security objectives determined in 6.2.
>
> The organization shall keep documented information to the extent necessary to have confidence that the processes have been carried out as planned.
>
> The organization shall control planned changes and review the consequences of unintended changes, taking action to mitigate any adverse effects, as necessary.
>
> The organization shall ensure that outsourced processes are determined and controlled.
>
> (ISO/IEC 27001:2013, 8.1)

4.5.1.2 Commentary

Operational planning, implementation and control relate back to Clauses 6.1 and 6.2 of ISO/IEC 27001:2013. This involves the organization planning, implementing and controlling its processes to meet its information security requirements, and implement the actions determined in 6.1, i.e.:

'...the risks and opportunities that need to be addressed to:

a) ensure the information security management system can achieve its intended outcome(s);
b) to prevent, or reduce, undesired effects; and
c) achieve continual improvement' (ISO/IEC 27001:2013, 6.1.1).

This also involves achieving the organization's information security objectives as specified in 6.2, i.e. to:

a) 'be consistent with the information security policy;
b) be measurable (if practicable);
c) take into account applicable information security requirements, and risk assessment and risk treatment results;
d) be communicated; and
e) be updated as appropriate' (ISO/IEC 27001:2013, 6.2).

Changes happen and this is an inevitable part of any business. The organization needs to monitor (9.1) and review (9.3) changes in external and internal issues that are relevant to the ISMS. An organization should plan and be prepared for change, control planned changes and review the consequences of unintended changes, taking action to mitigate any adverse effects, as necessary.

4.5.2 Information security risk assessment (8.2)

4.5.2.1 Requirements

> The organization shall perform information security risk assessments at planned intervals or when significant changes are proposed or occur, taking account of the criteria established in 6.1.2 a).
>
> The organization shall retain documented information of the results of the information security risk assessments.
>
> (ISO/IEC 27001:2013, 8.2)

4.5.2.2 Commentary

Internal changes to business processes and systems (such as technology changes) or external changes (such as new laws and regulations or new business environment) may create new information security risks. There is a multitude of ways in which changes could compromise information security and pose a risk to the organization. Therefore, the organization needs to keep up to date as regards the potential risks it faces and to stay 'ahead of the game' to ensure it can continue to protect its information assets and maintain an effective level of information security against these potential risks. This means the organization needs to carry out risk assessments at planned intervals to be 'ahead of the game', to ensure that the ISMS continues to be effective and to be able to protect its information assets. This re-assessment of the risks the organization faces may result in the need to formulate a revised treatment plan.

4.5.3 Information security risk treatment (8.3)

4.5.3.1 Requirements

'The organization shall implement the information security risk treatment plan.

The organization shall retain documented information of the results of the information security risk treatment' (ISO/IEC 27001:2013, 8.3).

4.5.3.2 Commentary

The organization shall now implement the risk treatment plans that were developed during the planning stage (ISO/IEC 27001:2013, 6.1.3) or after a re-assessment of the risks (ISO/IEC 27001:2013, 8.2).

4.6 Performance evaluation (Clause 9)

4.6.1 Monitoring, measurement, analysis and evaluation (9.1)

4.6.1.1 Requirements

> The organization shall evaluate the information security performance and the effectiveness of the information security management system.
>
> The organization shall determine:
>
> a) what needs to be monitored and measured, including information security processes and controls;
> b) the methods for monitoring, measurement, analysis and evaluation, as applicable, to ensure valid results;
> NOTE The methods selected should produce comparable and reproducible results to be considered valid.
> c) when the monitoring and measuring shall be performed;
> d) who shall monitor and measure;
> e) when the results from monitoring and measurement shall be analysed and evaluated; and

f) who shall analyse and evaluate these results.

The organization shall retain appropriate documented information as evidence of the monitoring and measurement results.

(ISO/IEC 27001:2013, 9.1)

4.6.1.2 Commentary

As part of the continual improvement process, the organization needs to monitor (9.1) the performance and effectiveness of its ISMS and subsequently provide input to the management review (9.3) of the ISMS. It is up to the organization what methods it uses to monitor, measure, analyse and evaluate the performance and effectiveness of its ISMS, and to make sure that the risk treatments it has implemented are 'ahead of the game' in terms of dealing with the ever changing risk and threat environment with which modern business is confronted. There are a number of guidelines that provide help with information security metrics and measurements, including ISO/IEC 27004[2] and BIP 0074.

4.6.2 Internal audit (9.2)

4.6.2.1 Requirements

The organization shall conduct internal audits at planned intervals to provide information on whether the information security management system:

a) conforms to
   1) the organization's own requirements for its information security management system; and
   2) the requirements of this International Standard;
b) is effectively implemented and maintained.

The organization shall:

c) plan, establish, implement and maintain an audit programme(s), including the frequency, methods, responsibilities, planning requirements and reporting. The audit programme(s) shall take into consideration the importance of the processes concerned and the results of previous audits;
d) define the audit criteria and scope for each audit;
e) select auditors and conduct audits that ensure objectivity and the impartiality of the audit process;

[2] At the time of publication of this guide, the valid edition of ISO/IEC 27004 is the 2009 version. However, this version is currently under revision and a new edition should appear in the next three to four years.

f) ensure that the results of the audits are reported to relevant management; and
g) retain documented information as evidence of the audit programme(s) and the audit results.

(ISO/IEC 27001:2013, 9.2)

4.6.2.2 Commentary

Internal ISMS audits (these are audits conducted by the organization, not third-party audits) are a mandatory requirement of 9.2 of ISO/IEC 27001:2013. The organization shall conduct ISMS audits to determine whether the control objectives, controls, procedures and processes fulfil the identified security requirements and comply with any applicable legislative, regulatory or contractual requirements. The ISMS audits shall also check whether the controls are effectively implemented and whether the control objectives, controls, procedures and processes perform as expected. The organization shall have plans in place regarding when these audits are to be conducted, and the responsibilities for planning and conducting the audits and the records of the results should be documented. The internal ISMS audits shall conform to the same requirements as any audit, such as impartiality of the auditor and documentation and reporting of results.

The results of the internal ISMS audits should be used to identify necessary improvements and provide input to internal management reviews (ISO/IEC 27001:2013, 9.3). Any nonconformity (ISO/IEC 27001:2013, 10.1) identified during the ISMS audits shall be eliminated as quickly as possible, and its cause identified and removed, to avoid recurrence, and the ISMS is to be improved (ISO/IEC 27001:2013, 10.2). There should be procedures in place to verify that the corrective actions (see 4.7.2) taken achieve their intended objective.

> [Internal] ISMS auditors should have knowledge and skills in the following areas:
>
> a) Information security management methods: to enable the auditor to examine ISMS and generate the appropriate audit findings and recommendations. Knowledge and skills in this area should include:
>   1) information security terminology;
>   2) information security management principles and their application; and
>   3) information security risk management methods and their application.
>
> b) General knowledge in information technology and information security techniques, as applicable (for example, physical and

logical access control techniques; protection against malicious software; vulnerability management techniques, etc.), or access thereto.

c) Current information security threats, vulnerabilities and controls, plus the broader organizational, legal and contractual context for the ISMS (e.g. changing business processes and relationships, technology or laws).

(ISO/IEC 27007:2011, 7.2.3.3.1)

ISO/IEC 27007 and ISO 19011 provide auditor guidance for first, second and third-party audits.

4.6.3 Management review (9.3)

4.6.3.1 Requirements

Top management shall review the organization's information security management system at planned intervals to ensure its continuing suitability, adequacy and effectiveness.

The management review shall include consideration of:

a) the status of actions from previous management reviews;
b) changes in external and internal issues that are relevant to the information security management system;
c) feedback on the information security performance, including trends in:
   1) nonconformities and corrective actions;
   2) monitoring and measurement results;
   3) audit results; and
   4) fulfilment of information security objectives;
d) feedback from interested parties;
e) results of risk assessment and status of risk treatment plan; and
f) opportunities for continual improvement.

(ISO/IEC 27001:2013, 9.3)

4.6.3.2 Commentary

It is important that the management shall review the organization's ISMS according to an established plan and review the programme in accordance with 9.3 of ISO/IEC 27001:2013 to ensure its continued adequacy and effectiveness. Review of the ISMS enables the organization to judge and assess whether improvements and changes are needed to the ISMS. The 'Performance evaluation' stage (see 4.6.1) stresses the importance of monitoring and reviewing changes to the business and operational environment of the ISMS and the current threat situation to identify and evaluate whether the ISMS is still valid and provides sufficient information security. After reviewing the situation, it may mean that some policies and procedures need to be added/changed/improved, some technical controls need to be added/changed/improved and so on. Without reviewing and auditing the ISMS on a regular basis it can become out of date, ineffective and inefficient in managing the risks the organization faces, and so eventually the situation occurs in which the organization is investing in an ISMS that is no longer useful or relevant.

There are various types of audit and review that an organization may need to consider: a first-party audit and review (e.g. an internal ISMS audit; see also 4.6.2), a second-party audit and review (e.g. as a customer requirement or part of a contractual arrangement) or a third-party audit and review (e.g. an ISMS certification carried out by an independent third-party certification body).

It is important that organizations make sure that sufficient and accurate information is input into the review process to enable the right decisions to be made and appropriate actions to be taken. If organizations are to go to the effort of having management reviews then it is important that sufficient information is available to make these right decisions to avoid wasting time and resource.

4.7 Improvement (Clause 10)

4.7.1 ISMS nonconformities (10.1)

4.7.1.1 Requirements

When a nonconformity occurs, the organization shall:

a) react to the nonconformity, and as applicable:
   1) take action to control and correct it; and
   2) deal with the consequences;
b) evaluate the need for action to eliminate the causes of nonconformity, in order that it does not recur or occur elsewhere, by:
   1) reviewing the nonconformity;
   2) determining the causes of the nonconformity; and
   3) determining if similar nonconformities exist, or could potentially occur;
c) implement any action needed;
d) review the effectiveness of any corrective action taken; and
e) make changes to the information security management system, if necessary.

(ISO/IEC 27001:2013, 10.1)

4.7.1.2 Commentary

The identification and resolution of nonconformities is an essential aspect of the continual improvement process. An ISMS non-conformity is a non-fulfilment of a requirement (e.g. ISO/IEC 27001, 6.1.3 d)).

Risk is constantly changing, being influenced by internal and external conditions. It is therefore necessary to manage it proactively with reviews being carried out in response to changes identified in the 'Performance evaluation' stage (Clause 9). The organization shall have processes in place to implement any identified ISMS improvements and to take corrective actions, as defined in ISO/IEC 27001:2013, 10.1.

4.7.2 Corrective actions and continual improvement (10.1 and 10.2)

4.7.2.1 Requirements

> Corrective actions shall be appropriate to the effects of the nonconformities encountered. The organization shall retain documented information as evidence of:
>
> f) the nature of the nonconformities and any subsequent actions taken; and
> g) the results of any corrective action.
>
> **10.2 Continual improvement**
>
> The organization shall continually improve the suitability, adequacy and effectiveness of the information security management system.
>
> (ISO/IEC 27001:2013, 10.1 to 10.2)

4.7.2.2 Commentary

The ISMS corrective actions shall be appropriate to the impact of the problems encountered. The procedures shall define requirements for:

a) identifying nonconformities (e.g. from management reviews and internal audits);
b) determining the causes of nonconformities;
c) correcting nonconformities;
d) evaluating the need for actions to ensure that nonconformities do not recur;
e) determining and implementing in a timely manner, the actions needed;
f) recording the results of actions taken; and
g) reviewing the effectiveness of corrective actions that have been taken.

5 ISMS certification

5.1 Overview

5.1.1 Certification of a management system

Certification of a management system provides independent demonstration that the management system of the organization:

a) conforms to specified requirements;
b) is capable of consistently achieving its stated policy and objectives; and
c) is effectively implemented.

The overall aim of certification is to give confidence to all parties that a management system fulfils specified requirements. The value of certification is the degree of public confidence and trust that is established by an impartial and competent assessment by a third party. Parties that have an interest in certification include, but are not limited to:

a) the clients of the certification bodies;
b) the customers of the organizations whose management systems are certified;
c) governmental authorities;
d) non-governmental organizations; and
e) consumers and other members of the public.

Certification of an organization's ISMS is a generally accepted way of providing an audit and assessment showing that the organization has implemented a management system of information security that meets the requirements specified in ISO/IEC 27001:2013. The certification process that applies to ISMS is the same as that deployed for other management systems, such as ISO 9001 (quality management system) and ISO/IEC 20000-1 (IT service management system) certification.

5.1.2 Definitions of accreditation and certification

Certification of management systems (ISO/IEC 17021:2011) is a third-party conformity assessment activity (see ISO/IEC 17000:2004, 5.5). Bodies performing this activity are therefore third-party conformity assessment bodies.

Note 1 Certification of a management system is sometimes also called 'registration' and certification bodies are sometimes called 'registrars'.

Note 2 A certification body can be non-governmental or governmental (with or without regulatory authority).

Third-party certification audit (ISO/IEC 17021:2011) is an audit carried out by an auditing organization independent of the client and the user, for the purpose of certifying the client's management system.

> NOTE 1 ...the term "audit" has been used for simplicity to refer to third-party certification audit.
>
> NOTE 2 Third-party certification audits include initial, surveillance, re-certification audits, and can also include special audits.
>
> NOTE 3 Third-party certification audits are typically conducted by audit teams of those bodies providing certification of conformity to the requirements of management system standards.
>
> NOTE 4 A joint audit is when two or more auditing organizations cooperate to audit a single client.
>
> NOTE 5 A combined audit is when a client is being audited against the requirements of two or more management systems standards together.
>
> NOTE 6 An integrated audit is when a client has integrated the application of requirements of two or more management systems standards into a single management system and is being audited against more than one standard.
>
> (ISO/IEC 17021:2011, 3.4)

5.1.3 Parties involved in ISMS certification

The certification process involves the following parties:

- **accreditation body**: a body responsible for assessing and accrediting certification/registration bodies to carry out certifications;
- **certification/registration body**: a third party that assesses and certifies the ISMS of a client organization with respect to published ISMS standards, and any supplementary documentation required under the system;
- **organization**: company, corporation, firm, enterprise, authority or institution, or part or combination thereof, whether incorporated or

not, public or private, that has its own functions and administration and is able to ensure that information security is exercised and whose management system is the subject of certification, and these are the clients of the certification bodies.

5.1.4 Accreditation and certification standards

Accreditation bodies have agreements and collaborate with each other through international[3] and regional[4] accreditation networks. The assessment activities of the accreditation bodies in relation to the certification bodies (CBs) and, in turn, the CBs' clients, are based on a number of standards and guides used for accreditation. For ISMS certification (in addition to the ISMS requirements standard ISO/IEC 27001:2013) these include:

- ISO 19011:2011, *Guidelines for auditing management systems*;
- ISO/IEC 17000:2004, *Conformity assessment — Vocabulary and general principles*;
- ISO/IEC 17021:2011, *Conformity assessment — Requirements for bodies providing audit and certification of management systems*;
- ISO/IEC 27006:2011, *Information technology — Security techniques — Requirements for bodies providing audit and certification of information security management systems*;
- ISO/IEC 27007: 2011 – *Information technology — Security techniques — Guidelines for information security management systems auditing.*

5.1.5 ISMS auditors and audit teams, and certification functions

Auditors carrying out ISMS assessments need to be qualified and have the appropriate experience and areas of competence as specified in several of the documents listed in 5.1.4 above. For example, Annex A of ISO/IEC 17021:2011 defines the generic requirements for auditor competence, and the specific ISMS requirements are covered in Clauses 7.1 to 7.3 and Annex B of ISO/IEC 27006:2011, and Clause 7 of ISO/IEC 27007. In addition, the ISMS audit team as a whole needs to have the combined skills and competence to cover the requirements of individual ISMS certifications, and it is up to the certification body to have a process and criteria in place for the selection of an audit team with such collective competence.

3 International Accreditation Forum (IAF).

4 European co-operation for Accreditation (EA), InterAmerican Accreditation Cooperation (IAAC), Pacific Accreditation Cooperation (PAC), Southern African Development Community Cooperation in Accreditation (SADCA).

As well as the competence requirements of auditors and audit teams, Annex B of ISO/IEC 27006:2011 provides a summary of the competence requirements for personnel involved in specific certification functions, for example, those that take the decision on granting/withdrawing a certification within the certification body.

The certification body shall have criteria for verifying:

- the background experience, specific training or briefing of audit teams that ensures knowledge of the ISMS standard and other relevant normative documents;
- knowledge of information security;
- knowledge of risk assessment and risk management from the business perspective; and
- technical knowledge of the activity to be audited.

Auditors shall be able to demonstrate their knowledge and experience, for example, through:

- recognized ISMS-specific qualifications;
- registration as an auditor;
- approved ISMS training courses; and/or
- up-to-date continuous professional development records.

The International Register of Certificated Auditors (IRCA) manages an ISMS auditor scheme, which enables auditors to be registered as qualified ISMS auditors if they meet the requirements defined in these standards (see http://www.irca.org). As part of the certification process, IRCA evaluates applicants against these requirements, which reflect the competence-defining key skills, knowledge and experience that the ISMS auditor needs to have and demonstrate during an audit. The evaluation criteria specify the education, work experience, auditor training and auditing experience an applicant needs to qualify for registration of these grades.

5.1.6 Certification

Accredited ISMS certification involves an assessment and audit of an organization's ISMS to check compliance with the requirements specified in ISO/IEC 27001:2013. This ISMS assessment and audit is carried out by an audit team (one or more auditors) deployed by the certification body to carry out this work. Details of what is involved are provided in 5.2, below.

If the ISMS assessment and audit is successful then the audit team will recommend to its certification body that a certificate should be awarded to the organization for its ISMS implementation. This recommendation is reviewed by a management team within the certification body (this team will be a different set of people from those who have carried out the audit). If the review is positive, then registration of the organization's ISMS will take place, and a certificate will be issued to the organization marked with the certification marks of the certification body and accreditation body.

Going for accredited certification of an ISMS is entirely voluntary – a business decision made by the organization. Organizations that successfully complete an ISO/IEC 27001:2013 certification can have greater confidence in their ability to manage information security, and this in turn will help them to assure and provide confidence to trading partners, customers and shareholders with whom they do business. The accredited ISO/IEC 27001:2013 ISMS certificate is a public statement of the organization's ISMS capability whilst allowing it to keep the specific details of its information security controls confidential.

5.1.7 Certificates

The certificate that is issued lasts for three years, after which the organization can apply for its ISMS to be re-assessed to obtain a certificate for another period of three years. For the three-year period during which the certificate is valid, the organization's ISMS is subject to a number of surveillance visits. These will involve the certification body's auditors carrying out checks to assess whether or not the ISMS is being kept up to date and whether or not changes that are being made to the ISMS are reflected in appropriate improvements commensurate with maintaining effective information security.

5.1.8 Preparing for certification

5.1.8.1 Demonstration and assessment of compliance

Accredited ISO/IEC 27001:2013 certification involves the assessment of an organization's ISMS based on the certification process described in 5.2 of this guide. Being ready for such an assessment means that an organization has established and implemented, and is operating, an ISMS in conformance with the requirements defined in ISO/IEC 27001:2013, Clauses 4 to 10. It is also important that the organization has documented the results of the activities involved in the establishment and implementation of its ISMS. For example, in establishing the ISMS it is necessary that the organization has carried out a risk assessment and has produced a risk assessment report showing the risks it has identified, and the analysis and evaluation it has undertaken in assessing these risks (6.1.2), and that the organization has followed these activities with a risk treatment activity (6.1.3). With this example in mind, the organization needs to demonstrate, as part of the certification audit, that it has undertaken these risk process activities appropriately in order to satisfy the requirements in ISO/IEC 27001:2013. In the same way, the organization will need to demonstrate, by presenting auditable evidence to the certification body's audit team, that it has gone through the other processes and requirements defined in ISO/IEC 27001:2013.

5.1.8.2 Auditable evidence

The organization needs to present evidence to the auditors that it has established and implemented an ISMS based on the requirements of ISO/IEC 27001:2013, and that this ISMS is operational. Such evidence should demonstrate that the organization has engaged in a systematic approach, from defining the ISMS scope through to the implementation of a system of management procedures and controls appropriate to the information security needs of the business. The approach taken should also demonstrate and display evidence that appropriate management decisions have been taken on how to deal with the risks faced, based on a well-founded risk management process. In addition, the organization should be able to provide evidence of the procedures it has put in place to monitor, review and improve the ISMS, and that these are understood by users and are being used in practice. The audit process should have the opportunity to examine this evidence to confirm that management has taken adequate steps and carried out suitable actions to provide information security that meets the security requirements determined by its risk assessments, by any business requirements, and applicable legal, regulatory and contractual obligations, and in accordance with what is specified in ISO/IEC 27001:2013.

5.1.8.3 Exclusions and risk acceptance

Any exclusion of management controls found to be necessary to satisfy the risk acceptance criteria need to be justified and supported by suitable evidence that the actions taken by management do not affect the organization's ability and/or responsibility to manage its information security risks appropriately, and that any associated risks have been knowingly and objectively accepted by those in management who have the executive responsibility for making such decisions and who are accountable for making such decisions.

5.1.8.4 Presentation of a documented management system

It is therefore important that the ISMS in place is operational and functioning effectively, and that it is supported by a documentation system, relevant records and any other forms of evidence that clearly show and confirm due compliance with ISO/IEC 27001:2013.

Note: The ISO/IEC 27001 certification audit process is directly related to a management system and does not imply that the organization has achieved specific levels of information security related to its IT systems, products or services.

The organization might choose to present such evidence to the certification auditors that such systems, products or services do provide certain levels of IT security as assessed by separate IT security product evaluation, but such evaluation results are not the main aim or objective of the certification process.

The certification audit process and related certification topics are defined in 5.2 to 5.11 of this guide. The material in these sections are based on text from ISO/IEC 17021:2011 and ISO/IEC 27006:2011, the two international certification standards that define the requirements for the audit process and other certification topics.

5.2 Certification audit process

5.2.1 Audit programme

9.1.1.1 An audit programme for the full certification cycle shall be developed to clearly identify the audit activity(ies) required to demonstrate that the client's management system fulfils the requirements for certification to the selected standard(s) or other normative document(s).

9.1.1.2 The audit programme shall include a two-stage initial audit, surveillance audits in the first and second years, and a recertification audit in the third year prior to expiration of certification. The three-year certification cycle begins with the certification or recertification decision. The determination of the audit programme and any subsequent adjustments shall consider the size of the client organization, the scope and complexity of its management system, products and processes as well as a demonstrated level of management system effectiveness and the results of any previous audits.

(ISO/IEC 17021:2011, 9.1.1.1 and 9.1.1.2)

5.2.2 Audit objectives, scope and criteria

9.1.2.2.1 The audit objectives shall be determined by the certification body. The audit scope and criteria, including any changes, shall be established by the certification body after discussion with the client.

9.1.2.2.2 The audit objectives shall describe what is to be accomplished by the audit and shall include the following:

a) determination of the conformity of the client's management system, or parts of it, with audit criteria;

b) evaluation of the ability of the management system to ensure the client organization meets applicable statutory, regulatory and contractual requirements;

NOTE A management system certification audit is not a legal compliance audit.

c) evaluation of the effectiveness of the management system to ensure the client organization is continually meeting its specified objectives;
d) as applicable, identification of areas for potential improvement of the management system.

9.1.2.2.3 The audit scope shall describe the extent and boundaries of the audit, such as physical locations, organizational units, activities and processes to be audited. Where the initial or re-certification process consists of more than one audit (e.g. covering different locations), the scope of an individual audit may not cover the full certification scope, but the totality of audits shall be consistent with the scope in the certification document....

9.1.2.2.4 The audit criteria shall be used as a reference against which conformity is determined, and shall include:

- the requirements of a defined normative document on management systems;
- the defined processes and documentation of the management system developed by the client.

(ISO/IEC 17021:2011, 9.1.2.2.1 to 9.1.2.2.4)

Note: In the case of ISMS, the normative document is ISO/IEC 27001:2013.

5.2.3 Audit plan

The audit plan shall be appropriate to the objectives and the scope of the audit. The audit plan shall at least include or refer to the following:

a) the audit objectives;
b) the audit criteria;
c) the audit scope, including identification of the organizational and functional units or processes to be audited;
d) the dates and sites where the on-site audit activities are to be conducted, including visits to temporary sites, as appropriate;
e) the expected time and duration of on-site audit activities;
f) the roles and responsibilities of the audit team members and accompanying persons.

(ISO/IEC 17021:2011, 9.1.2.3)

5.2.4 Audit team

The certification body selects and appoints '...the audit team, including the audit team leader, taking into account the competence needed to achieve the objectives of the audit. If there is only one auditor, the auditor shall have the competence to perform the duties of an audit team leader applicable for that audit' (ISO/IEC 17021:2011, 9.1.3.1).

> The necessary knowledge and skills of the audit team leader and auditors may be supplemented by technical experts, translators and interpreters who shall operate under the direction of an auditor. Where translators or interpreters are used, they are to be selected such that they do not unduly influence the audit.
>
> NOTE The criteria for the selection of technical experts are determined on a case-by-case basis by the needs of the audit team and the scope of the audit.
>
> (ISO/IEC 17021:2011, 9.1.3.3)

ISO/IEC 17021:2011 provides more details regarding audit team selection.

5.2.5 Audit time

> The certification body shall have documented procedures for determining audit time, and for each client the certification body shall determine the time needed to plan and accomplish a complete and effective audit of the client's management system. The audit time determined by the certification body, and the justification for the determination, shall be recorded. In determining the audit time, the certification body shall consider, among other things, the following aspects:
>
> a) the requirements of the relevant management system standard;
> b) size and complexity;
> c) technological and regulatory context;
> d) any outsourcing of any activities included in the scope of the management system;
> e) the results of any prior audits;
> f) number of sites and multi-site considerations;
> g) the risks associated with the products, processes or activities of the organization;
> h) when audits are combined, joint or integrated.
>
> (ISO/IEC 17021:2011, 9.1.4.1)

ISO/IEC 27006:2011 provides additional information regarding the determination of audit time by the certification body as it relates to ISMS audits, including determining the complexity of the ISMS (ISO/IEC 27006:2011, Annex A) and calculation of the audit time of the ISMS (ISO/IEC 27006:2011, Annex C).

5.2.6 Multiple sites

Where multi-site sampling is utilized for the audit of a client's management system covering the same activity in various locations, the certification body shall develop a sampling programme to ensure proper audit of the management system. The rationale for the sampling plan shall be documented for each client.

(ISO/IEC 17021:2011, 9.1.5)

5.2.7 Communication of audit team tasks

The tasks given to the audit team shall be defined and shall be made known to the client organization, and shall require the audit team to

a) examine and verify the structure, policies, processes, procedures, records and related documents of the client organization relevant to the management system,
b) determine that these meet all the requirements relevant to the intended scope of certification,
c) determine that the processes and procedures are established, implemented and maintained effectively, to provide a basis for confidence in the client's management system, and
d) communicate to the client, for its action, any inconsistencies between the client's policy, objectives and targets (consistent with the expectations in the relevant management system standard or other normative document) and the results.

(ISO/IEC 17021:2011, 9.1.6)

5.2.8 Communication concerning audit team members

The certification body shall provide the name of and, when requested, make available background information on each member of the audit team, with sufficient time for the client organization to object to the appointment of any particular auditor or technical expert and for the certification body to reconstitute the team in response to any valid objection.

(ISO/IEC 17021:2011, 9.1.7)

5.2.9 Communication of audit plan

'The audit plan shall be communicated and the dates of the audit shall be agreed upon, in advance, with the client organization.'

(ISO/IEC 17021:2011, 9.1.8)

5.2.10 Conducting on-site audits

5.2.10.1 General

On-site audits '...shall include an opening meeting at the start of the audit and a closing meeting at the conclusion of the audit.'

(ISO/IEC 17021:2011, 9.1.9.1)

5.2.10.2 Conducting the opening meeting

A formal opening meeting, where attendance shall be recorded, shall be held with the client's management and, where appropriate, those responsible for the functions or processes to be audited. The purpose of the opening meeting, which shall usually be conducted by the audit team leader, is to provide a short explanation of how the audit activities will be undertaken and shall include the following elements. The degree of detail shall be consistent with the familiarity of the client with the audit process:

a) introduction of the participants, including an outline of their roles;
b) confirmation of the scope of certification;
c) confirmation of the audit plan (including type and scope of audit, objectives and criteria), any changes, and other relevant arrangements with the client, such as the date and time for the closing meeting, interim meetings between the audit team and the client's management;
d) confirmation of formal communication channels between the audit team and the client;
e) confirmation that the resources and facilities needed by the audit team are available;
f) confirmation of matters relating to confidentiality;
g) confirmation of relevant work safety, emergency and security procedures for the audit team;
h) confirmation of the availability, roles and identities of any guides and observers;

i) the method of reporting, including any grading of audit findings;
j) information about the conditions under which the audit may be prematurely terminated;
k) confirmation that the audit team leader and audit team representing the certification body is responsible for the audit and shall be in control of executing the audit plan including audit activities and audit trails;....

(ISO/IEC 17021:2011, 9.1.9.2)

5.2.10.3 Communication during the audit

9.1.9.3.1 During the audit, the audit team shall periodically assess audit progress and exchange information. The audit team leader shall reassign work as needed between the audit team members and periodically communicate the progress of the audit and any concerns to the client.

9.1.9.3.2 Where the available audit evidence indicates that the audit objectives are unattainable or suggests the presence of an immediate and significant risk (e.g. safety), the audit team leader shall report this to the client and, if possible, to the certification body to determine appropriate action. Such action may include reconfirmation or modification of the audit plan, changes to the audit objectives or audit scope, or termination of the audit. The audit team leader shall report the outcome of the action taken to the certification body.

9.1.9.3.3 The audit team leader shall review with the client any need for changes to the audit scope which becomes apparent as on-site auditing activities progress and report this to the certification body.

(ISO/IEC 17021:2011, 9.1.9.3.1 to 9.1.9.3.3)

5.2.10.4 Observers and guides

The presence and justification of observers during an audit activity shall be agreed to by the certification body and client prior to the conduct of the audit. The audit team shall ensure that observers do not influence or interfere in the audit process or outcome of the audit.

NOTE Observers can be members of the client's organization, consultants, witnessing accreditation body personnel, regulators or other justified persons.

(ISO/IEC 17021:2011, 9.1.9.4.1)

Each auditor shall be accompanied by a guide, unless otherwise agreed to by the audit team leader and the client. Guide(s) are assigned to the audit team to facilitate the audit. The audit team shall ensure that guides do not influence or interfere in the audit process or outcome of the audit.

NOTE The responsibilities of a guide can include:

a) establishing contacts and timing for interviews;
b) arranging visits to specific parts of the site or organization;
c) ensuring that rules concerning site safety and security procedures are known and respected by the audit team members;
d) witnessing the audit on behalf of the client;
e) providing clarification or information as requested by an auditor.

(ISO/IEC 17021:2011, 9.1.9.4.2)

5.2.10.5 Collecting and verifying information

9.1.9.5.1 During the audit, information relevant to the audit objectives, scope and criteria (including information relating to interfaces between functions, activities and processes) shall be collected by appropriate sampling and verified to become audit evidence.

9.1.9.5.2 Methods to collect information shall include, but are not limited to:

a) interviews;
b) observation of processes and activities;
c) review of documentation and records.

(ISO/IEC 17021:2011, 9.1.9.5.1 and 9.1.9.5.2)

5.2.10.6 Identifying and recording audit findings

9.1.9.6.1 Audit findings summarizing conformity and detailing nonconformity and its supporting audit evidence shall be recorded and reported to enable an informed certification decision to be made or the certification to be maintained.

9.1.9.6.2 Opportunities for improvement may be identified and recorded, unless prohibited by the requirements of a management system certification scheme. Audit findings, however, which are nonconformities in accordance with 9.1.15 b) and c) shall not be recorded as opportunities for improvement.

9.1.9.6.3 A finding of nonconformity shall be recorded against a specific requirement of the audit criteria, contain a clear statement of the nonconformity and identify in detail the objective evidence on which the nonconformity is based. Nonconformities shall be discussed with the client to ensure that the evidence is accurate and that the nonconformities are understood. The auditor however shall refrain from suggesting the cause of nonconformities or their solution.

NOTE Nonconformities, consistent with the requirements of 9.1.15 b), can be classified as major, whereas other nonconformities [9.1.15 c)] can be classified as minor nonconformities.

9.1.9.6.4 The audit team leader shall attempt to resolve any diverging opinions between the audit team and the client concerning audit evidence or findings, and unresolved points shall be recorded.

(ISO/IEC 17021:2011, 9.1.9.6.1 to 9.1.9.6.4)

5.2.10.7 Preparing audit conclusions

Prior to the closing meeting, the audit team shall:

a) review the audit findings, and any other appropriate information collected during the audit, against the audit objectives;
b) agree upon the audit conclusions, taking into account the uncertainty inherent in the audit process;
c) identify any necessary follow-up actions;
d) confirm the appropriateness of the audit programme or identify any modification required (e.g. scope, audit time or dates, surveillance frequency, competence).

(ISO/IEC 17021:2011, 9.1.9.7)

5.2.10.8 Conducting the closing meeting

9.1.9.8.1 A formal closing meeting, where attendance shall be recorded, shall be held with the client's management and, where appropriate, those responsible for the functions or processes audited. The purpose of the closing meeting, which shall normally be conducted by the audit team leader, is to present the audit conclusions, including the recommendation regarding certification. Any nonconformities shall be presented in such a manner that they are understood, and the timeframe for responding shall be agreed.

NOTE "Understood" does not necessarily mean that the nonconformities have been accepted by the client.

9.1.9.8.2 The closing meeting shall also include the following elements. The degree of detail shall be consistent with the familiarity of the client with the audit process:

a) advising the client that the audit evidence collected was based on a sample of the information; thereby introducing an element of uncertainty;
b) the method and timeframe of reporting, including any grading of audit findings;
c) the certification body's process for handling nonconformities including any consequences relating to the status of the client's certification;
d) the timeframe for the client to present a plan for correction and corrective action for any nonconformities identified during the audit;
e) the certification body's post audit activities;
f) information about the complaint handling and appeal processes.

9.1.9.8.3 The client shall be given opportunity for questions. Any diverging opinions regarding the audit findings or conclusions between the audit team and the client shall be discussed and resolved where possible. Any diverging opinions that are not resolved shall be recorded and referred to the certification body.

(ISO/IEC 17021:2011, 9.1.9.8.1 to 9.1.9.8.3)

5.2.11 Audit report

9.1.10.1 The certification body shall provide a written report for each audit. The audit team may identify opportunities for improvement but shall not recommend specific solutions. Ownership of the audit report shall be maintained by the certification body.

9.1.10.2 The audit team leader shall ensure that the audit report is prepared and shall be responsible for its content. The audit report shall provide an accurate, concise and clear record of the audit to enable an informed certification decision to be made and shall include or refer to the following:

a) identification of the certification body;
b) the name and address of the client and the client's management representative;
c) the type of audit (e.g. initial, surveillance or recertification audit);
d) the audit criteria;
e) the audit objectives;
f) the audit scope, particularly identification of the organizational or functional units or processes audited and the time of the audit;
g) identification of the audit team leader, audit team members and any accompanying persons;

h) the dates and places where the audit activities (on site or offsite) were conducted;
i) audit findings, evidence and conclusions, consistent with the requirements of the type of audit;
j) any unresolved issues, if identified.

(ISO/IEC 17021:2011, 9.1.10.1 and 9.1.10.2)

5.2.12 Cause analysis of nonconformities

'The certification body shall require the client to analyse the cause and describe the specific correction and corrective actions taken, or planned to be taken, to eliminate detected nonconformities, within a defined time.'

(ISO/IEC 17021:2011, 9.1.11)

5.2.13 Effectiveness of corrections and corrective actions

The certification body shall review the corrections, identified causes and corrective actions submitted by the client to determine if these are acceptable. The certification body shall verify the effectiveness of any correction and corrective actions taken. The evidence obtained to support the resolution of nonconformities shall be recorded. The client shall be informed of the result of the review and verification.

NOTE Verification of effectiveness of correction and corrective action can be carried out based on a review of documentation provided by the client, or where necessary, through verification on-site.

(ISO/IEC 17021:2011, 9.1.12)

5.2.14 Additional audits

'The client shall be informed if an additional full audit, an additional limited audit, or documented evidence (to be confirmed during future surveillance audits) will be needed to verify effective correction and corrective actions.'

(ISO/IEC 17021:2011, 9.1.13)

5.2.15 Certification decision

'The certification body shall ensure that the persons or committees that make the certification or recertification decisions are different from those who carried out the audits.'

(ISO/IEC 17021:2011, 9.1.14)

5.2.16 Actions prior to making a decision

The certification body shall confirm, prior to making a decision, that

a) the information provided by the audit team is sufficient with respect to the certification requirements and the scope for certification;
b) it has reviewed, accepted and verified the effectiveness of correction and corrective actions, for all nonconformities that represent
    1) failure to fulfil one or more requirements of the management system standard, or
    2) a situation that raises significant doubt about the ability of the client's management system to achieve its intended outputs;
c) it has reviewed and accepted the client's planned correction and corrective action for any other nonconformities.

(ISO/IEC 17021:2011, 9.1.15)

5.3 Initial audit and certification

'The initial certification audit of a [information security] management system shall be conducted in two stages: stage 1 and stage 2.'

(ISO/IEC 17021:2011, 9.2.3)

5.3.1 Application

The certification body shall require an authorized representative of the applicant organization to provide the necessary information to enable it to establish the following:

a) the desired scope of the certification;
b) the general features of the applicant organization, including its name and the address(es) of its physical location(s), significant aspects of its process and operations, and any relevant legal obligations;

c) general information, relevant for the field of certification applied for, concerning the applicant organization, such as its activities, human and technical resources, functions and relationship in a larger corporation, if any;
d) information concerning all outsourced processes used by the organization that will affect conformity to requirements;
e) the standards or other requirements for which the applicant organization is seeking certification;
f) information concerning the use of consultancy relating to the management system.

(ISO/IEC 17021:2011, 9.2.1)

5.3.2 Application review

9.2.2.1 Before proceeding with the audit, the certification body shall conduct a review of the application and supplementary information for certification to ensure that

a) the information about the applicant organization and its management system is sufficient for the conduct of the audit;
b) the requirements for certification are clearly defined and documented, and have been provided to the applicant organization;
c) any known difference in understanding between the certification body and the applicant organization is resolved;
d) the certification body has the competence and ability to perform the certification activity;
e) the scope of certification sought, the location(s) of the applicant organization's operations, time required to complete audits and any other points influencing the certification activity are taken into account (language, safety conditions, threats to impartiality, etc.);
f) records of the justification for the decision to undertake the audit are maintained.

9.2.2.2 Following the review of the application, the certification body shall either accept or decline an application for certification. When the certification body declines an application for certification as a result of the review of application, the reasons for declining an application shall be documented and made clear to the client.

NOTE When declining an application for certification, the certification body should be careful not to act in conflict with the principles set out in Clause 4.

9.2.2.3 Based on this review, the certification body shall determine the competences it needs to include in its audit team and for the certification decision.

9.2.2.4 The audit team shall be appointed and composed of auditors (and technical experts, as necessary) who, between them, have the totality of the competences identified by the certification body as set out in 9.2.2.3 for the certification of the applicant organization. The selection of the team shall be performed with reference to the designations of competence of auditors and technical experts made under 7.2.5, and may include the use of both internal and external human resources.

9.2.2.5 The individual(s) who will be conducting the certification decision shall be appointed to ensure appropriate competence is available....

(ISO/IEC 17021:2011, 9.2.2.1 to 9.2.2.5)

5.3.3 Initial certification audit

5.3.3.1 ISMS stage 1 audit

The general objectives of the stage 1 audit as specified in ISO/IEC 17021:2011 shall be to:

a) audit the client's management system documentation;
b) evaluate the client's location and site-specific conditions and to undertake discussions with the client's personnel to determine the preparedness for the stage 2 audit;
c) review the client's status and understanding regarding requirements of the standard, in particular with respect to the identification of key performance or significant aspects, processes, objectives and operation of the management system;
d) collect necessary information regarding the scope of the management system, processes and location(s) of the client, and related statutory and regulatory aspects and compliance (e.g. quality, environmental, legal aspects of the client's operation, associated risks, etc.);
e) review the allocation of resources for stage 2 audit and agree with the client on the details of the stage 2 audit;
f) provide a focus for planning the stage 2 audit by gaining a sufficient understanding of the client's management system and site operations in the context of possible significant aspects;
g) evaluate if the internal audits and management review are being planned and performed, and that the level of implementation of the management system substantiates that the client is ready for the stage 2 audit.

(ISO/IEC 17021:2011, 9.2.3.1.1)

As regards ISMS certification audits, 9.2.3.1 of ISO/IEC 27006:2011 gives the following additional guidance to that given in ISO/IEC 17021:2011:

> In this stage of the audit, the certification body shall obtain documentation on the design[5] of the ISMS...[as] required in...ISO/IEC 27001.
>
> The objective of the stage 1 audit is to provide a focus for planning the stage 2 audit by gaining an understanding of the ISMS in the context of the client organization's ISMS policy and objectives, and, in particular, of the client organization's state of preparedness for the audit.
>
> The stage 1 audit shall include, but should not be restricted to, the document review. The certification body shall agree with the client organization when and where the document review is conducted. In every case, the document review shall be completed prior to the commencement of the stage 2 audit.
>
> The results of the stage 1 audit shall be documented in a written report. The certification body shall review the stage 1 audit report before deciding on proceeding with the stage 2 audit and for selecting the stage 2 audit team members with the necessary competence.
>
> The certification body shall make the client organization aware of the further types of information and records that may be required for detailed examination during the stage 2 audit.
>
> (ISO/IEC 27006:2011, 9.2.3.1)

5.3.3.2 ISMS stage 2 audit

5.3.3.2.1 General purpose

The general objectives of the stage 2 audit, as specified in ISO/IEC 17021:2011, 9.2.3.2 shall be '...to evaluate the implementation, including effectiveness, of the client's management system'. According to ISO/IEC 17021:2011:

> The stage 2 audit shall take place at the site(s) of the client. It shall include at least the following:

[5] [Note: Documents relevant to the design of the ISMS should cover at least the organization's risk assessment report, risk treatment plan and the Statement of Applicability, and other core elements of the ISMS.]

a) information and evidence about conformity to all requirements of the applicable management system standard or other normative document;
b) performance monitoring, measuring, reporting and reviewing against key performance objectives and targets (consistent with the expectations in the applicable management system standard or other normative document);
c) the client's management system and performance as regards legal compliance;
d) operational control of the client's processes;
e) internal auditing and management review;
f) management responsibility for the client's policies;
g) links between the normative requirements, policy, performance objectives and targets (consistent with the expectations in the applicable management system standard or other normative document), any applicable legal requirements, responsibilities, competence of personnel, operations, procedures, performance data and internal audit findings and conclusions.

(ISO/IEC 17021:2011, 9.2.3.2)

5.3.3.2.2. ISMS-specific purpose

As regards ISMS certification audits 9.2.3.2.1 of ISO/IEC 27006:2011 gives the following additional guidance to that given in ISO/IEC 17021:2011:

The [ISMS] stage 2 audit always takes place at the site(s) of the client organization. On the basis of findings documented in the [ISMS] stage 1 audit report, the certification body drafts an audit plan for the conduct of the [ISMS] stage 2 audit. The objectives of the [ISMS] stage 2 audit are

a) to confirm that the client organization adheres to its own policies, objectives and procedures;
b) to confirm that the ISMS conforms to all the requirements of the normative ISMS standard ISO/IEC 27001 and is achieving the client organization's policy objectives.

(ISO/IEC 27006:2011, 9.2.3.2.1)

5.3.3.2.3. ISMS focus

The ISMS stage 2

...audit shall focus on the client organization's

a) assessment of information security related risks, and that the assessments produce comparable and reproducible results;
b) documentation requirements listed in...ISO/IEC 27001;

c) selection of control objectives and controls based on the risk assessment and risk treatment processes;
d) reviews of the effectiveness of the ISMS and measurements of the effectiveness of the information security controls, reporting and reviewing against the ISMS objectives;
e) internal ISMS audits and management reviews;
f) management responsibility for the information security policy;
g) correspondence between the selected and implemented controls, the Statement of Applicability, and the results of the risk assessment and risk treatment process, and the ISMS policy and objectives;
h) implementation of controls (see Annex D), taking into account the organization's measurements of effectiveness of controls [see d) above], to determine whether controls are implemented and effective to achieve the stated objectives;
i) programmes, processes, procedures, records, internal audits, and reviews of the ISMS effectiveness to ensure that these are traceable to management decisions and the ISMS policy and objectives.

(ISO/IEC 27006:2011, 9.2.3.2.2)

5.3.3.2.4. ISMS scope

ISO/IEC 27006:2011 defines the following requirements regarding the ISMS scope.

> The audit team shall audit the ISMS of the client organization covered by the defined scope against all applicable certification requirements. The certification body shall ensure that the scope and boundaries of the ISMS of the client organization are clearly defined in terms of the characteristics of the business, the organization, its location, assets and technology. The certification body shall confirm, in the scope of their ISMS, that client organizations address the requirements stated in...[Clause 4.1.3 of ISO/IEC 27001:2013].
>
> Certification bodies shall ensure that the client organization's information security risk assessment and risk treatment properly reflects its activities and extends to the boundaries of its activities as defined in the ISMS standard ISO/IEC 27001[:2013]. Certification bodies shall confirm that this is reflected in the client organization's scope of their ISMS and Statement of Applicability [singular per scope].

Certification bodies shall ensure that interfaces with services or activities that are not completely within the scope of the ISMS are addressed within the ISMS subject to certification and are included in the client organization's information security risk assessment. An example of such a situation is the sharing of facilities (e.g. IT systems, databases and telecommunication systems [or the outsourcing of a business function]) with other organizations.

(ISO/IEC 27006:2011, 9.1.2)

5.3.4 Initial certification audit conclusions

'The audit team shall analyse all information and audit evidence gathered during the stage 1 and stage 2 audits to review the audit findings and agree on the audit conclusions.'

(ISO/IEC 17021:2011, 9.2.4)

5.3.5 Information for granting initial certification

9.2.5.1 The information provided by the audit team to the certification body for the certification decision shall include, as a minimum,

a) the audit reports,
b) comments on the nonconformities and, where applicable, the correction and corrective actions taken by the client,
c) confirmation of the information provided to the certification body used in the application review (see 9.2.2), and
d) a recommendation whether or not to grant certification, together with any conditions or observations.

9.2.5.2 The certification body shall make the certification decision on the basis of an evaluation of the audit findings and conclusions and any other relevant information (e.g. public information, comments on the audit report from the client).

(ISO/IEC 17021:2011, 9.2.5.1 and 9.2.5.2)

5.4 Surveillance activities

5.4.1 General

9.3.1.1 The certification body shall develop its surveillance activities so that representative areas and functions covered by the scope of the management system are monitored on a regular basis, and take into account changes to its certified client and its management system.

9.3.1.2 Surveillance activities shall include on-site audits assessing the certified client's management system's fulfilment of specified requirements with respect to the standard to which the certification is granted. Other surveillance activities may include

a) enquiries from the certification body to the certified client on aspects of certification,
b) reviewing any client's statements with respect to its operations (e.g. promotional material, website),
c) requests to the client to provide documents and records (on paper or electronic media), and
d) other means of monitoring the certified client's performance.

(ISO/IEC 17021:2011, 9.3.1.1 and 9.3.1.2)

5.4.2 Surveillance audits

5.4.2.1 Surveillance audit programme

9.3.2.1 Surveillance audits are on-site audits, but are not necessarily full system audits, and shall be planned together with the other surveillance activities so that the certification body can maintain confidence that the certified management system continues to fulfil requirements between recertification audits. The surveillance audit programme shall include, at least

a) internal audits and management review,
b) a review of actions taken on nonconformities identified during the previous audit,
c) treatment of complaints,
d) effectiveness of the management system with regard to achieving the certified client's objectives,
e) progress of planned activities aimed at continual improvement,
f) continuing operational control,
g) review of any changes, and
h) use of marks and/or any other reference to certification.

9.3.2.2 Surveillance audits shall be conducted at least once a year. The date of the first surveillance audit following initial certification shall not be more than 12 months from the last day of the stage 2 audit.

(ISO/IEC 17021:2011, 9.3.2.1 and 9.3.2.2)

5.4.2.2 Purpose of surveillance audit

The purpose of surveillance is to verify that the approved ISMS continues to be implemented, to consider the implications of changes to that system initiated as a result of changes in the client organization's operation and to confirm continued compliance with certification requirements. Surveillance audit programmes shall cover:

a) the system maintenance elements which are [risk assessment and control maintenance,] internal ISMS audit, management review and preventive and corrective action;
b) communications from external parties as required by the ISMS standard ISO/IEC 27001 and other documents required for certification;
c) changes to the documented system;
d) areas subject to change;
e) selected elements of ISO/IEC 27001;
f) other selected areas as appropriate.

(ISO/IEC 27006:2011, 9.3.1.1)

5.4.2.3 Scope of review

As a minimum, [every] surveillance by the certification body shall review the following:

a) the effectiveness of the ISMS with regard to achieving the objectives of the client organization's information security policy;
b) the functioning of procedures for the periodic evaluation and review of compliance with relevant information security legislation and regulations;
c) action taken on nonconformities identified during the last audit....

(ISO/IEC 27006:2011, 9.3.1.2)

In addition to what is covered above regarding the requirements of ISO/IEC 17021:2011 (see 5.4.1 and 5.4.2.1), the following issues shall be covered.

a) The certification body shall be able to adapt its surveillance programme to the information security issues related .... to the client organization and justify this programme.[6]
b) The surveillance programme of the certification body shall be determined by the certification body. Specific dates for visits may be agreed with the certified client organization.
c) Surveillance audits may be combined with audits of other management systems. The reporting shall clearly indicate the aspects relevant to each management system.
d) The certification body shall supervise the appropriate use of the certificate.

During surveillance audits, certification bodies shall check the records of appeals and complaints brought before the certification body and, where any nonconformity or failure to meet the requirements of certification is revealed, that the client organization has investigated its own ISMS and procedures and taken appropriate corrective action.

A surveillance report shall contain, in particular, information on clearing of nonconformities revealed previously [and the version of, and control selection in, the Statement of Applicability]. As a minimum, the reports arising from surveillance shall build up to cover in totality the requirement of point a) above.

(ISO/IEC 27006:2011, 9.3.1.3)

5.4.3 Maintaining certification

The certification body shall maintain certification based on demonstration that the client continues to satisfy the requirements of the management system standard. It may maintain a client's certification based on a positive conclusion by the audit team leader without further independent review, provided

a) for any nonconformity or other situation that may lead to suspension or withdrawal of certification, the certification body has a system that requires the audit team leader to report to the

[6] The 2011 version of ISO/IEC 27006 states 'The certification body shall be able to adapt its surveillance programme to the information security issues related threats to assets, vulnerabilities and impacts on to the client organization and justify this programme.' ISO/IEC 27006 is currently undergoing revision to bring it in line with the ISO 17021 revision and the 2013 edition of ISO/IEC 27001. It is no longer a requirement of the 2013 edition of ISO/IEC 27001 to identify the assets, threats and vulnerabilities during the risk assessment phase, so 5.4.2.3 (a) is modified from the ISO/IEC 27006 requirement. During the certification transition period the audit will need to take account of the original ISO/IEC 27006 requirement and the 2013 edition of ISO/IEC 27001. After the transition period the requirements of the 2013 edition of ISO/IEC 27001 apply and so a revised version of ISO/IEC 27006:2011, 5.4.2.3 (a) will apply (as yet not yet defined).

certification body the need to initiate a review by appropriately competent personnel (see 7.2.9), different from those who carried out the audit, to determine whether certification can be maintained, and

b) competent personnel of the certification body monitor its surveillance activities, including monitoring the reporting by its auditors, to confirm that the certification activity is operating effectively.

(ISO/IEC 17021:2011, 9.3.3)

5.5 Recertification

5.5.1 Recertification audit planning

9.4.1.1 A recertification audit shall be planned and conducted to evaluate the continued fulfilment of all of the requirements of the relevant management system standard or other normative document. The purpose of the recertification audit is to confirm the continued conformity and effectiveness of the management system as a whole, and its continued relevance and applicability for the scope of certification.

9.4.1.2 The recertification audit shall consider the performance of the management system over the period of certification, and include the review of previous surveillance audit reports.

9.4.1.3 Recertification audit activities may need to have a stage 1 audit in situations where there have been significant changes to the management system, the client, or the context in which the management system is operating (e.g. changes to legislation).

9.4.1.4 In the case of multiple sites or certification to multiple management system standards being provided by the certification body, the planning for the audit shall ensure adequate on-site audit coverage to provide confidence in the certification.

(ISO/IEC 17021:2011, 9.4.1.1 to 9.4.1.4)

5.5.2 Recertification audit

9.4.2.1 The recertification audit shall include an on-site audit that addresses the following:

a) the effectiveness of the management system in its entirety in the light of internal and external changes and its continued relevance and applicability to the scope of certification;
b) demonstrated commitment to maintain the effectiveness and improvement of the management system in order to enhance overall performance;
c) whether the operation of the certified management system contributes to the achievement of the organization's policy and objectives.

9.4.2.2 When, during a recertification audit, instances of nonconformity or lack of evidence of conformity are identified, the certification body shall define time limits for correction and corrective actions to be implemented prior to the expiration of certification.

(ISO/IEC 17021:2011, 9.4.2.1 and 9.4.2.2)

9.4.3 The certification body shall make decisions on renewing certification based on the results of the recertification audit, as well as the results of the review of the system over the period of certification and complaints received from users of certification.

(ISO/IEC 17021:2011, 9.4.3)

If on surveillance or recertification audit, nonconformities are found to exist, such nonconformities shall be effectively corrected within a time agreed by the certification body. If correction is not made within the time agreed the scope of certification shall be reduced, or the certificate suspended or withdrawn. The time allowed to implement corrective action shall be consistent with the severity of the nonconformity and the risk to the assurance of products or services of the client organization meeting specified requirements.

(ISO/IEC 27006:2011, 9.4.1).

5.6 Special audits

5.6.1 Extensions to scope

The certification body shall, in response to an application for extension to the scope of a certification already granted, undertake a review of the application and determine any audit activities necessary to decide whether or not the extension may be granted. This may be conducted in conjunction with a surveillance audit.

(ISO/IEC 17021:2011, 9.5.1)

5.6.2 Short-notice audits

It may be necessary for the certification body to conduct audits of certified clients at short notice to investigate complaints (see 9.8), or in response to changes (see 8.6.3), or as follow up on suspended clients (see 9.6). In such cases

a)the certification body shall describe and make known in advance to the certified clients (e.g. in documents as described in 8.6.1) the conditions under which these short notice visits are to be conducted, and

b)the certification body shall exercise additional care in the assignment of the audit team because of the lack of opportunity for the client to object to audit team members.

(ISO/IEC 17021:2011, 9.5.2)

5.7 Suspending, withdrawing or reducing the scope of certification

9.6.2 The certification body shall suspend certification in cases when, for example,

- the client's certified management system has persistently or seriously failed to meet certification requirements, including requirements for the effectiveness of the management system,
- the certified client does not allow surveillance or recertification audits to be conducted at the required frequencies, or
- the certified client has voluntarily requested a suspension.

9.6.3 Under suspension, the client's management system certification is temporarily invalid. The certification body shall have enforceable arrangements with its clients to ensure that in case of suspension the client refrains from further promotion of its certification. The certification body shall make the suspended status of the certification publicly accessible (see 8.1.3) and shall take any other measures it deems appropriate.

9.6.4 Failure to resolve the issues that have resulted in the suspension in a time established by the certification body shall result in withdrawal or reduction of the scope of certification.

NOTE In most cases the suspension would not exceed 6 months.

9.6.5 The certification body shall reduce the client's scope of certification to exclude the parts not meeting the requirements, when the client has persistently or seriously failed to meet the certification requirements for those parts of the scope of certification. Any such reduction shall be in line with the requirements of the standard used for certification.

9.6.6 The certification body shall have enforceable arrangements with the certified client concerning conditions of withdrawal [see 8.4.3 d)] ensuring upon notice of withdrawal of certification that the client discontinues its use of all advertising matter that contains any reference to a certified status.

9.6.7 Upon request by any party, the certification body shall correctly state the status of certification of a client's management system as being suspended, withdrawn or reduced.

(ISO/IEC 17021:2011, 9.6.2 to 9.6.7)

5.8 Appeals

'The certification body shall have a documented process to receive, evaluate and make decisions on appeals.'

(ISO/IEC 17021:2011, 9.7)

For more details of the appeals process consult 9.7 of ISO/IEC 17021:2011.

5.9 Complaints

9.8.4 The certification body shall have a documented process to receive, evaluate and make decisions on complaints. This process shall be subject to requirements for confidentiality, as it relates to the complainant and to the subject of the complaint.

(ISO/IEC 17021:2011, 9.8.4)

9.8.2 Upon receipt of a complaint, the certification body shall confirm whether the complaint relates to certification activities that it is responsible for and, if so, shall deal with it. If the complaint relates to a certified client, then examination of the complaint shall consider the effectiveness of the certified management system.

(ISO/IEC 17021:2011, 9.8.2)

For more details of the complaints process consult 9.8 of ISO/IEC 17021:2011.

5.10 Records of applicants and clients

9.9.1 The certification body shall maintain records on the audit and other certification activities for all clients, including all organizations that submitted applications, and all organizations audited, certified, or with certification suspended or withdrawn.

9.9.2 Records on certified clients shall include the following:

a) application information and initial, surveillance and recertification audit reports;
b) certification agreement;
c) justification of the methodology used for sampling;
d) justification for auditor time determination (see 9.1.4);
e) verification of correction and corrective actions;
f) records of complaints and appeals, and any subsequent correction or corrective actions;
g) committee deliberations and decisions, if applicable;
h) documentation of the certification decisions;
i) certification documents, including the scope of certification with respect to product, process or service, as applicable;
j) related records necessary to establish the credibility of the certification, such as evidence of the competence of auditors and technical experts.

NOTE Methodology of sampling includes the sampling employed to assess the specific management system and/or to select sites in the context of multi-site assessment.

9.9.3 The certification body shall keep the records on applicants and clients secure to ensure that the information is kept confidential. Records shall be transported, transmitted or transferred in a way that ensures that confidentiality is maintained.

(ISO/IEC 17021:2011, 9.9.1 to 9.9.3)

5.11 Other related topics

5.11.1 Certification documents

8.2.1 The certification body shall provide certification documents to the certified client by any means it chooses.

8.2.2 The effective date on a certification document shall not be before the date of the certification decision.

8.2.3 The certification document(s) shall identify the following:

a) the name and geographic location of each client whose management system is certified (or the geographic location of the headquarters and any sites within the scope of a multi-site certification);
b) the dates of granting, extending or renewing certification;
c) the expiry date or recertification due date consistent with the recertification cycle;
d) a unique identification code;
e) the standard and/or other normative document, including issue number and/or revision, used for audit of the certified client;
f) the scope of certification with respect to product (including service), process, etc., as applicable at each site;
g) the name, address and certification mark of the certification body; other marks (e.g. accreditation symbol) may be used provided they are not misleading or ambiguous;
h) any other information required by the standard and/or other normative document used for certification;
i) in the event of issuing any revised certification documents, a means to distinguish the revised documents from any prior obsolete documents.

(ISO/IEC 17021:2011, 8.2.1 to 8.2.3)

Note: In the case of ISMS certification audits, the normative document referred to in e) above is ISO/IEC 27001.

5.11.2 Reference to certification and use of marks

A certification body shall have a policy governing any mark that it authorizes certified clients to use. This shall assure, among other things, traceability back to the certification body. There shall be no ambiguity, in the mark or accompanying text, as to what has been certified and which certification body has granted the certification. This mark shall not be used on a product or product packaging seen by the consumer or in any other way that may be interpreted as denoting product conformity.

NOTE ISO/IEC 17030 provides requirements for use of third-party marks.

(ISO/IEC 17021:2011, 8.4.1)

8.4.3 The certification body shall require that the client organization

a) conforms to the requirements of the certification body when making reference to its certification status in communication media such as the internet, brochures or advertising, or other documents,

b) does not make or permit any misleading statement regarding its certification,
c) does not use or permit the use of a certification document or any part thereof in a misleading manner,
d) upon suspension or withdrawal of its certification, discontinues its use of all advertising matter that contains a reference to certification, as directed by the certification body (see 9.6.3 and 9.6.6),
e) amends all advertising matter when the scope of certification has been reduced,
f) does not allow reference to its management system certification to be used in such a way as to imply that the certification body certifies a product (including service) or process,
g) does not imply that the certification applies to activities that are outside the scope of certification, and
h) does not use its certification in such a manner that would bring the certification body and/or certification system into disrepute and lose public trust.

8.4.4 The certification body shall exercise proper control of ownership and shall take action to deal with incorrect references to certification status or misleading use of certification documents, marks or audit reports.

(ISO/IEC 17021:2011, 8.4.3 and 8.4.4)

5.11.3 Confidentiality

Before the certification audit, the certification body shall ask the client organization to report if any ISMS records cannot be made available for review by the audit team because they contain confidential or sensitive information. The certification body shall determine whether the ISMS can be adequately audited in the absence of these records. If the certification body concludes that it is not possible to adequately audit the ISMS without reviewing the identified confidential or sensitive records, it shall advise the client organization that the certification audit cannot take place until appropriate access arrangements are granted.

(ISO/IEC 27006:2011, 8.5.1)

5.11.4 Information exchange between a certification body and its clients

5.11.4.1 Certification activities

The certification body shall provide and update clients on the following:

a) a detailed description of the initial and continuing certification activity, including the application, initial audits, surveillance audits, and the process for granting, maintaining, reducing, extending, suspending, withdrawing certification and recertification;
b) the normative requirements for certification;
c) information about the fees for application, initial certification and continuing certification;
d) the certification body's requirements for prospective clients to
   1) comply with certification requirements,
   2) make all necessary arrangements for the conduct of the audits, including provision for examining documentation and the access to all processes and areas, records and personnel for the purposes of initial certification, surveillance, recertification and resolution of complaints, and
   3) make provisions, where applicable, to accommodate the presence of observers (e.g. accreditation auditors or trainee auditors);
e) documents describing the rights and duties of certified clients, including requirements, when making reference to its certification in communication of any kind in line with the requirements in 8.4;
f) information on procedures for handling complaints and appeals.

(ISO/IEC 17021:2011, 8.6.1)

5.11.4.2 Notice of changes by a certification body

The certification body shall give its certified clients due notice of any changes to its requirements for certification. The certification body shall verify that each certified client complies with the new requirements.

NOTE Contractual arrangements with certified clients could be necessary to ensure implementation of these requirements. A model of a license agreement for the use of certification, including the aspects related to a notice of changes, as far as applicable, is found in Annex E of ISO/IEC Guide 28:2004.

(ISO/IEC 17021:2011, 8.6.2)

5.11.4.3 Notice of changes by a client

The certification body shall have legally enforceable arrangements to ensure that the certified client informs the certification body, without delay, of matters that may affect the capability of the management system to continue to fulfil the requirements of the standard used for certification. These include, for example, changes relating to

a) the legal, commercial, organizational status or ownership,
b) organization and management (e.g. key managerial, decision-making or technical staff),
c) contact address and sites,
d) scope of operations under the certified management system, and
e) major changes to the management system and processes.

NOTE A model of a license agreement for the use of certification, including the aspects related to a notice of changes, as far as applicable, is found in Annex E of ISO/IEC Guide 28:2004.

(ISO/IEC 17021:2011, 8.6.3)

5.11.5 Integrated management systems

5.11.5.1 Integration of ISMS documentation with that for other management systems

The certification body may accept documentation that is combined (e.g. for information security, '...quality, health and safety, and environment) as long as the ISMS can be clearly identified together with the appropriate interfaces to the other systems.'

(ISO/IEC 27006:2011, 9.2.3.3.2)

5.11.5.2 Combining management system audits

'A certification body may offer other management system certification linked with the ISMS certification, or may offer ISMS certification only.'

(ISO/IEC 27006:2011, 9.2.3.3.3)

Annex A

Mapping Old – New Editions of ISO/IEC 27001 and ISO/IEC 27002 (ISO/IEC JTC 1/SC27/WG1 Standing Document SD3)

Introduction

The purpose of SD3 is to show the corresponding relationship between the 2005 and 2013 versions of ISO/IEC 27001 and ISO/IEC 27002.

Both standards have been revised as part of the normal standards maintenance process, and the results of this revision process are contained in FDIS ISO/IEC 27001:2013 and FDIS ISO/IEC 27002:2013.

This Standing Document contains the following tables:

- Table A: Comparison between ISO/IEC 27001:2013 and ISO/IEC 27001:2005
- Table B: Comparison between ISO/IEC 27002:2005 and ISO/IEC 27002:2013
- Table C: Comparison between ISO/IEC 27002:2013 and ISO/IEC 27002:2005

These tables can be used to determine where requirements or controls in the old standards went, or where requirements or controls in the new standards have come from. Where a relationship is stated, it does not mean that the content is identical. Users of this document can evaluate the significance of the changes in their context.

NOTE: This document is designed to be purely a factual correspondence between the old and new editions of ISO/IEC 27001 and ISO/IEC 27002 respectively, and so by intention it does not provide any explanatory commentary on why changes have been made. For ISO/IEC 27002, the comparison was based on control objectives, controls, and implementation guidance.

Target Audience

This document will be useful to users migrating from the 2005 versions to the 2013 versions of ISO/IEC 27001 and ISO/IEC 27002. This includes those intending to upgrade their ISO/IEC 27001 for certification purposes.

Certification Transition Arrangements

The International Accreditation Forum (IAF) at its General Assembly meeting on October 24th and 25th 2013 made the following statement:

- The General Assembly, acting on the recommendation of the Technical Committee, resolved to endorse ISO/IEC 27001:2013 as a normative document.
- The General Assembly further agreed that the deadline for conformance to ISO/IEC 27001:2013 will be two years from the date of publication.
- One year after publication of ISO/IEC 27001:2013, all new accredited certifications issued shall be to ISO/IEC 27001:2013.

Note: As the date of publication was 1 October 2013, the deadline for Certification Bodies to conform will be 1 October 2015.

Table A: Comparison between ISO/IEC 27001:2013 and ISO/IEC 27001:2005

ISO/IEC 27001:2013	ISO/IEC 27001:2005
4.1 Understanding the organization and its context	8.3 Preventive action
4.2 a) Understanding the needs and expectations of interested parties	New requirement
4.2 b) Understanding the needs and expectations of interested parties	5.2.1 c) Provision of resources 7.3 c) 4) Review output 7.3 c) 5) Review output
4.3 Determining the scope of the information security management system	4.2.1 a) Establish the ISMS
4.3 a) Determining the scope of the information security management system	4.2.1 a) Establish the ISMS 4.2.3 f) Monitor and review the ISMS
4.3 b) Determining the scope of the information security management system	4.2.3 f) Monitor and review the ISMS
4.3 c) Determining the scope of the information security management system	New requirement
4.3 Determining the scope of the information security management system – Last sentence	4.3.1 b) General 4.3.2 f) Control of documents
4.4 Information security management system	4.1 General requirements 5.2.1 a) Provision of resources
5.1 a) Leadership and commitment	4.2.1 b) 3) Establish the ISMS 5.1 a), b) Management commitment
5.1 b) Leadership and commitment	New requirement
5.1 c) Leadership and commitment	5.1 e) Management commitment
5.1 d) Leadership and commitment	5.1 d) Management commitment

ISO/IEC 27001:2013	ISO/IEC 27001:2005
5.1 e) Leadership and commitment	5.1 b), g), h) Management commitment
5.1 f) Leadership and commitment	5.1 b), g), h) Management commitment
5.1 g) Leadership and commitment	5.1 a), d), g), h) Management commitment
5.1 h) Leadership and commitment	5.1 Management commitment
5.2 Policy – First sentence	4.2.1 b) 5) Establish the ISMS 5.1 a) Management commitment
5.2 a) Policy	4.2.1 b) Establish the ISMS
5.2 b) Policy	4.2.1 b) 1) Establish the ISMS
5.2 c) Policy	4.2.1 2) Establish the ISMS 4.3.3 Control of records
5.2 d) Policy	5.1 d) Management commitment
5.2 e) Policy	4.3.1 a) General
5.2 f) Policy	5.1 d) Management commitment
5.2 g) Policy	4.3.2 f) Control of documents
5.3 Organizational roles, responsibilities and authorities - First sentence	5.1 c) Management commitment 6 Internal ISMS audits
5.3 a) Organizational roles, responsibilities and authorities	4.3.3 Control of records 5.1 c) Management commitment 6 Internal ISMS audits
5.3 b) Organizational roles, responsibilities and authorities	4.3.3 Control of records

ISO/IEC 27001:2013	ISO/IEC 27001:2005
	5.1 c) Management commitment 6 Internal ISMS audits
6.1.1 Actions to address risks and opportunities – General	4.2.1 d) Establish the ISMS 8.3 a) Preventive action
6.1.1 a) Actions to address risks and opportunities – General	New requirement
6.1.1 b) Actions to address risks and opportunities - General	New requirement
6.1.1 c) Actions to address risks and opportunities - General	New requirement
6.1.1 d) Actions to address risks and opportunities - General	4.2.1 e) 4) Establish the ISMS 8.3 b), c) Preventive action
6.1.1 e) 1) Actions to address risks and opportunities - General	4.2.2 a) Implement and operate the ISMS 8.3 c) Preventive action
6.1.1 e) 2) Actions to address risks and opportunities - General	8.3 e) Preventive action
6.1.2 Information security risk assessment - First sentence	4.2.1 c) 1) Establish the ISMS
6.1.2 a) Information security risk assessment	New requirement
6.1.2 a) 1) Information security risk assessment	4.2.1 b) 4), c) 2) Establish the ISMS 5.1 f) Management commitment
6.1.2 a) 2) Information security risk assessment	New requirement
6.1.2 b) Information security risk assessment	4.2.1 c) Establish the ISMS
6.1.2 c) Information security risk assessment	4.2.1 d) Establish the ISMS

ISO/IEC 27001:2013	ISO/IEC 27001:2005
6.1.2 c) 1) Information security risk assessment	4.2.1 d) 1), 2), 3), 4) Establish the ISMS
6.1.2 c) 2) Information security risk assessment	4.2.1 d) 1) Establish the ISMS
6.1.2 d) 1) Information security risk assessment	4.2.1 e) 1) Establish the ISMS
6.1.2 d) 2) Information security risk assessment	4.2.1 e) 2) Establish the ISMS
6.1.2 d) 3) Information security risk assessment	4.2.1 e) 3) Establish the ISMS
6.1.2 e) 1) Information security risk assessment	4.2.1 e) 4) Establish the ISMS
6.1.2 e) 2) Information security risk assessment	4.2.1 e) 4) Establish the ISMS
6.1.2 Information security risk assessment - Last sentence	4.3.1 d), e) General
6.1.3 Information security risk treatment	4.2.1 f) Establish the ISMS
6.1.3 a) Information security risk treatment	4.2.1 f) 1), 2), 3), 4) Establish the ISMS
6.1.3 b) Information security risk treatment	4.2.1 g) Establish the ISMS
6.1.3 c) Information security risk treatment	New requirement
6.1.3 d) Information security risk treatment	4.2.1 j) 1), 2), 3) Establish the ISMS 4.3.1 i) General
6.1.3 e) Information security risk treatment	4.2.2 a) Implement and operate the ISMS
6.1.3 f) Information security risk treatment	4.2.1 h) Establish the ISMS
6.1.3 Information security risk treatment - Last sentence	4.3.1 f) General

ISO/IEC 27001:2013	ISO/IEC 27001:2005
6.2 Information security objectives and plans to achieve them - First sentence	5.1 b) Management commitment
6.2 a) Information security objectives and plans to achieve them	5.1 d) Management commitment
6.2 b) Information security objectives and plans to achieve them	New requirement
6.2 c) Information security objectives and plans to achieve them	New requirement
6.2 d) Information security objectives and plans to achieve them	5.1 d) Management commitment
6.2 e) Information security objectives and plans to achieve them	4.2.3 b) Monitor and review the ISMS
6.2 Information security objectives and plans to achieve them - Last sentence	4.3.1 a) General
6.2 f) Information security objectives and plans to achieve them	New requirement
6.2 g) Information security objectives and plans to achieve them	New requirement
6.2 h) Information security objectives and plans to achieve them	New requirement
6.2 i) Information security objectives and plans to achieve them	New requirement
6.2 j) Information security objectives and plans to achieve them	4.2.3 b) Monitor and review the ISMS
7.1 Resources	4.2.2 b), g) Implement and operate the ISMS 5.2.1 Provision of resources
7.2 a) Competence	5.2.2 a) Training, awareness and competence
7.2 b) Competence	5.2.2 Training, awareness and competence

ISO/IEC 27001:2013	ISO/IEC 27001:2005
7.2 c) Competence	5.2.2 b), c) Training, awareness and competence
7.2 d) Competence	5.2.2 d) Training, awareness and competence
7.3 a) Awareness	New requirement
7.3 b) Awareness	4.2.2 e) Implement and operate the ISMS 5.2.2 Training, awareness and competence
7.3 c) Awareness	4.2.2 e) Implement and operate the ISMS 5.2.2 Training, awareness and competence
7.4 Communication - First sentence	4.2.4 c) Maintain and improve the ISMS 5.1 d) Management commitment
7.4 a) Communication	4.2.4 c) Maintain and improve the ISMS 5.1 d) Management commitment
7.4 b) Communication	New requirement
7.4 c) Communication	4.2.4 c) Maintain and improve the ISMS 5.1 d) Management commitment
7.4 d) Communication	New requirement
7.4 e) Communication	New requirement
7.5.1 a) General	4.3.1 a), b), h), i) General
7.5.1 b) General	New requirement

ISO/IEC 27001:2013	ISO/IEC 27001:2005
7.5.2 a) Creating and updating	4.3.2 c), e), j) Control of documents 4.3.3 Control of records
7.5.2 b) Creating and updating	New requirement
7.5.2 c) Creating and updating	4.3.2 a), b) Control of documents
7.5.3 Control of documented information - First sentence	4.3.2 Control of documents
7.5.3 a) Control of documented information	4.3.2 d), f) Control of documents 4.3.3 Control of records
7.5.3 b) Control of documented information	4.3.2 Control of documents 4.3.3 Control of records
7.5.3 c) Control of documented information	4.3.2 f), h) i) Control of documents 4.3.3 Control of records
7.5.3 d) Control of documented information	4.3.2 f), h) Control of documents 4.3.3 Control of records
7.5.3 e) Control of documented information	4.3.2 c), d) Control of documents
7.5.3 f) Control of documented information	4.3.2 f), j) Control of documents 4.3.3 Control of records
7.5.3 Control of documented information - Last paragraph	4.3.2 g) Control of documents
8.1 Operational planning and control-First paragraph-first sentence	New requirement
8.1 Operational planning and control-First paragraph-second sentence	4.2.2 c) Implement controls selected

ISO/IEC 27001:2013	ISO/IEC 27001:2005
	f) Implement and operate the ISMS
8.1 Operational planning and control - Second paragraph	4.3.3 Control of records
8.1 Operational planning and control - Third paragraph	New requirement
8.1 Operational planning and control - Last paragraph	4.2.2 h) Implement and operate the ISMS 8.3 b), c) Preventive action
8.2 Information security risk assessment	4.2.3 d) Monitor and review the ISMS 4.3.1 e) General
8.3 Information security risk treatment	4.2.2 b), c) Implement and operate the ISMS 4.3.3 Control of records
9.1 Monitoring, measurement, analysis and evaluation - First paragraph	4.2.3 b), c) Monitor and review the ISMS 6 d) Internal ISMS audits
9.1 a) Monitoring, measurement, analysis and evaluation	4.2.3 a), c), d), g) Monitor and review the ISMS
9.1 b) Monitoring, measurement, analysis and evaluation	4.2.2 d) Implement and operate the ISMS
9.1 c) Monitoring, measurement, analysis and evaluation	New requirement
9.1 d) Monitoring, measurement, analysis and evaluation	New requirement
9.1 e) Monitoring, measurement, analysis and evaluation	4.2.3 b) Monitor and review the ISMS
9.1 f) Monitoring, measurement, analysis and evaluation	New requirement

ISO/IEC 27001:2013	ISO/IEC 27001:2005
9.1 Monitoring, measurement, analysis and evaluation - Last paragraph	4.2.3 h) Monitor and review the ISMS 4.3.3 Control of records
9.2 Internal audit-First paragraph	4.2.3 e) Monitor and review the ISMS 6 Internal ISMS audits
9.2 a) 1) Internal audit	6 b) Internal ISMS audits
9.2 a) 2) Internal audit	6 a) Internal ISMS audits
9.2 b) Internal audit	6 c) Internal ISMS audits
9.2 c) Internal audit	6 Internal ISMS audits
9.2 d) Internal audit	6 Internal ISMS audits
9.2 e) Internal audit	6 Internal ISMS audits
9.2 f) Internal audit	6 Internal ISMS audits
9.2 g) Internal audit	4.3.1 h) General 4.3.3 Control of records 6 Internal ISMS audits
9.3 Management review - First paragraph	4.2.3 f) Monitor and review the ISMS 5.1 h) Management commitment 5.2.1 e) Provision of resources 7.1 General
9.3 a) Management review	7.2 g) Review input
9.3 b) Management review	4.2.3 d) 1), 2), 3), 4), 5), 6) Monitor and review the ISMS 7.2 c), e), h) Review input
9.3 c) Management review	7.2 f) Review input

ISO/IEC 27001:2013	ISO/IEC 27001:2005
9.3 c) 1) Management review	7.2 d) Review input
9.3 c) 2) Management review	7.2 f) Review input
9.3 c) 3) Management review	7.2 a) Review input
9.3 c) 4) Management review	New requirement
9.3 d) Management review	7.2 b) Review input
9.3 e) Management review	7.2 e), f) Review input
9.3 f) Management review	7.2 i) Review input
9.3 Management review - Penultimate paragraph	4.2.3 d), g) Monitor and review the ISMS 7.1 General 7.3 Review output
9.3 Management review - Last paragraph	4.3.3 Control of records 7.1 General
10.1 a) Nonconformity and corrective action	8.2 Corrective action
10.1 a) 1) Nonconformity and corrective action	8.2 Corrective action
10.1 a) 2) Nonconformity and corrective action	8.2 Corrective action
10.1 b) Nonconformity and corrective action	8.2 c) Corrective action 8.3 b) Preventive action
10.1 b) 1) Nonconformity and corrective action	8.2 a) Corrective action
10.1 b) 2) Nonconformity and corrective action	8.2 b) Corrective action
10.1 b) 3) Nonconformity and corrective action	8.2 a) Corrective action 8.3 a) Preventive action

ISO/IEC 27001:2013	ISO/IEC 27001:2005
10.1 c) Nonconformity and corrective action	4.2.4 b) Maintain and improve the ISMS 8.2 d) Corrective action
10.1 d) Nonconformity and corrective action	8.2 f) Corrective action
10.1 e) Nonconformity and corrective action	New requirement
10.1 Nonconformity and corrective action - Last paragraph	New requirement
10.1 f) Nonconformity and corrective action	8.2 b), c), d) Corrective action
10.1 g) Nonconformity and corrective action	8.2 e) Corrective action
10.2 Continual improvement	4.2.4 a), b) d) Maintain and improve the ISMS 5.2.1 f) Provision of resources 8.1 Continual improvement

REQUIREMENTS DELETED FROM ISO/IEC 27001:2005 BY CLAUSE

4.2.1, 4.2.1 i), 4.2.3 a) 1), 4.2.3 a) 2), 4.2.3 a) 4),4.2.3 a) 5), 4.2.3 h), 4.3.1, 4.3.1 c), 4.3.2, 4.3.3, 5.2.1 b), 5.2.1 d), 8.3 d), 8.3

Table B: Comparison between ISO/IEC 27002:2005 and ISO/IEC 27002:2013

ISO/IEC 27002:2005	ISO/IEC 27002:2013
5 Security policy	
5.1 Information security policy	5.1 Management direction for information security
5.1.1 Information security policy document	5.1.1 Policies for information security
5.1.2 Review of the information security policy	5.1.2 Review of the policies for information security
6 Organization of information security	
6.1 Internal organization	
6.1.1 Management commitment to information security	7.2.1 Management responsibilities
6.1.2 Information security co-ordination	Deleted
6.1.3 Allocation of information security responsibilities	6.1.1 Information security roles and responsibilities
6.1.4 Authorization process for information processing facilities	Deleted
6.1.5 Confidentiality agreements	13.2.4 Confidentiality or nondisclosure agreements
6.1.6 Contact with authorities	6.1.3 Contact with authorities
6.1.7 Contact with special interest groups	6.1.4 Contact with special interest groups
6.1.8 Independent review of information security	18.2.1 Independent review of information security
6.2 External parties	
6.2.1 Identification of risks related to external parties	Deleted

ISO/IEC 27002:2005	ISO/IEC 27002:2013
6.2.2 Addressing security when dealing with customers	Deleted
6.2.3 Addressing security in third party agreements	15.1.2 Addressing security within supplier agreements
7 Asset management	
7.1 Responsibility for assets	
7.1.1 Inventory of assets	8.1.1 Inventory of assets
7.1.2 Ownership of assets	8.1.2 Ownership of assets
7.1.3 Acceptable use of assets	8.1.3 Acceptable use of assets
7.2 Information classification	
7.2.1 Classification guidelines	8.2.1 Classification of Information
7.2.2 Information labelling and handling	8.2.2 Labelling of information 8.2.3 Handling of assets
8 Human resources security	
8.1 Prior to employment	
8.1.1 Roles and responsibilities	6.1.1 Information security roles and responsibilities
8.1.2 Screening	7.1.1 Screening
8.1.3 Terms and conditions of employment	7.1.2 Terms and conditions of employment
8.2 During employment	
8.2.1 Management responsibilities	7.2.1 Management responsibilities
8.2.2 Information security awareness, education and training	7.2.2 Information security awareness, education and training
8.2.3 Disciplinary process	7.2.3 Disciplinary process

ISO/IEC 27002:2005	ISO/IEC 27002:2013
8.3 Termination or change of employment	
8.3.1 Termination responsibilities	7.3.1 Termination or change of employment responsibilities
8.3.2 Return of assets	8.1.4 Return of assets
8.3.3 Removal of access rights	9.2.6 Removal or adjustment of access rights
9 Physical and environmental security	
9.1 Secure areas	
9.1.1 Physical security perimeter	11.1.1 Physical security perimeter
9.1.2 Physical entry controls	11.1.2 Physical entry controls
9.1.3 Securing offices, rooms and facilities	11.1.3 Securing offices, rooms and facilities
9.1.4 Protecting against external and environmental threats	11.1.4 Protecting against external and environmental threats
9.1.5 Working in secure areas	11.1.5 Working in secure areas
9.1.6 Public access, delivery and loading areas	11.1.6 Delivery and loading areas
9.2 Equipment security	
9.2.1 Equipment siting and protection	11.2.1 Equipment siting and protection
9.2.2 Supporting utilities	11.2.2 Supporting utilities
9.2.3 Cabling security	11.2.3 Cabling security
9.2.4 Equipment maintenance	11.2.4 Equipment maintenance
9.2.5 Security of equipment off-premises	11.2.6 Security of equipment and assets off-premises

ISO/IEC 27002:2005	ISO/IEC 27002:2013
9.2.6 Secure disposal or re-use of equipment	11.2.7 Secure disposal or re-use of equipment
9.2.7 Removal of property	11.2.5 Removal of assets
10 Communications and operations management	
10.1 Operational procedures and responsibilities	
10.1.1 Documented operating procedures	12.1.1 Documented operating procedures
10.1.2 Change management	12.1.2 Change management
10.1.3 Segregation of duties	6.1.2 Segregation of duties
10.1.4 Separation of development, test and operational facilities	12.1.4 Separation of development, testing and operational environments
10.2 Third party service delivery management	
10.2.1 Service delivery	15.2.1 Monitoring and review of supplier services
10.2.2 Monitoring and review of third party services	15.2.1 Monitoring and review of supplier services
10.2.3 Managing changes to third party services	15.2.2 Managing changes to supplier services
10.3 System planning and acceptance	
10.3.1 Capacity management	12.1.3 Capacity management
10.3.2 System acceptance	14.2.9 System acceptance testing
10.4 Protection against malicious and mobile code	
10.4.1 Controls against malicious code	12.2.1 Controls against malware

ISO/IEC 27002:2005	ISO/IEC 27002:2013
10.4.2 Controls against mobile code	Deleted
10.5 Back-up	
10.5.1 Information back-up	12.3.1 Information backup
10.6 Network security management	
10.6.1 Network controls	13.1.1 Network controls
10.6.2 Security of network services	13.1.2 Security of network services
10.7 Media handling	
10.7.1 Management of removable media	8.3.1 Management of removable media
10.7.2 Disposal of media	8.3.2 Disposal of media
10.7.3 Information handling procedures	8.2.3 Handling of assets
10.7.4 Security of system documentation	
10.8 Exchange of information	
10.8.1 Information exchange policies and procedures	13.2.1 Information transfer policies and procedures
10.8.2 Exchange agreements	13.2.2 Agreements on information transfer
10.8.3 Physical media in transit	8.3.3 Physical media transfer
10.8.4 Electronic messaging	13.2.3 Electronic messaging
10.8.5 Business information systems	Deleted
10.9 Electronic commerce services	

ISO/IEC 27002:2005	ISO/IEC 27002:2013
10.9.1 Electronic commerce	14.1.2 Securing application services on public networks
10.9.2 On-line transactions	14.1.3 Protecting application services transactions
10.9.3 Publicly available information	Deleted
10.10 Monitoring	
10.10.1 Audit logging	12.4.1 Event logging
10.10.2 Monitoring system use	Deleted
10.10.3 Protection of log information	12.4.2 Protection of log information
10.10.4 Administrator and operator logs	12.4.3 Administrator and operator logs
10.10.5 Fault logging	12.4.1 Event logging
10.10.6 Clock synchronization	12.4.4 Clock synchronization
11 Access control	
11.1 Business requirement for access control	
11.1.1 Access control policy	9.1.1 Access control policy
11.2 User access management	
11.2.1 User registration	9.2.1 User registration and deregistration 9.2.2 User access provisioning
11.2.2 Privilege management	9.2.3 Management of privileged access rights
11.2.3 User password management	9.2.4 Management of secret authentication information of users
11.2.4 Review of user access rights	9.2.5 Review of user access rights

ISO/IEC 27002:2005	ISO/IEC 27002:2013
11.3 User responsibilities	
11.3.1 Password use	9.3.1 Use of secret authentication information
11.3.2 Unattended user equipment	11.2.8 Unattended user equipment
11.3.3 Clear desk and clear screen policy	11.2.9 Clear desk and clear screen policy
11.4 Network access control	
11.4.1 Policy on use of network services	9.1.2 Access to networks and network services
11.4.2 User authentication for external connections	Deleted
11.4.3 Equipment identification in networks	13.1.1 Network controls
11.4.4 Remote diagnostic and configuration port protection	Deleted
11.4.5 Segregation in networks	13.1.3 Segregation in networks
11.4.6 Network connection control	Deleted
11.4.7 Network routing control	Deleted
11.5 Operating system access control	
11.5.1 Secure log-on procedures	9.4.2 Secure log-on procedures
11.5.2 User identification and authentication	9.2.1 User registration and deregistration 9.2.2 User access provisioning
11.5.3 Password management system	9.4.3 Password management system
11.5.4 Use of system utilities	9.4.4 Use of privileged utility programs
11.5.5 Session time-out	9.4.2 Secure log-on procedures

ISO/IEC 27002:2005	ISO/IEC 27002:2013
11.5.6 Limitation of connection time	9.4.2 Secure log-on procedures
11.6 Application and information access control	
11.6.1 Information access restriction	9.4.1 Information access restriction
11.6.2 Sensitive system isolation	9.4.1 Information access restriction
11.7 Mobile computing and teleworking	
11.7.1 Mobile computing and communications	6.2.1 Mobile device policy
11.7.2 Teleworking	6.2.2 Teleworking
12 Information systems acquisition, development and maintenance	
12.1 Security requirements of information systems	
12.1.1 Security requirements analysis and specification	14.1.1 Information security requirements analysis and specification
12.2 Correct processing in applications	
12.2.1 Input data validation	Deleted
12.2.2 Control of internal processing	Deleted
12.2.3 Message integrity	Deleted
12.2.4 Output data validation	Deleted
12.3 Cryptographic controls	
12.3.1 Policy on the use of cryptographic controls	10.1.1 Policy on the use of cryptographic controls

ISO/IEC 27002:2005	ISO/IEC 27002:2013
12.3.2 Key management	10.1.2 Key management
12.4 Security of system files	
12.4.1 Control of operational software	12.5.1 Installation of software on operational systems 12.6.2 Restrictions on software installation
12.4.2 Protection of system test data	14.3.1 Protection of test data
12.4.3 Access control to program source code	9.4.5 Access control to program source code
12.5 Security in development and support processes	
12.5.1 Change control procedures	14.2.2 System change control procedures
12.5.2 Technical review of applications after operating system changes	14.2.3 Technical review of applications after operating platform changes
12.5.3 Restrictions on changes to software packages	14.2.4 Restrictions on changes to software packages
12.5.4 Information leakage	Deleted
12.5.5 Outsourced software development	14.2.7 Outsourced development
12.6 Technical vulnerability management	
12.6.1 Control of technical vulnerabilities	12.6.1 Management of technical vulnerabilities
13 Information security incident management	
13.1 Reporting information security events and weaknesses	
13.1.1 Reporting information security events	16.1.2 Reporting information security events

ISO/IEC 27002:2005	ISO/IEC 27002:2013
13.1.2 Reporting security weaknesses	16.1.3 Reporting information security weaknesses
13.2 Management of information security incidents and improvements	
13.2.1 Responsibilities and procedures	16.1.1 Responsibilities and procedures
13.2.2 Learning from information security incidents	16.1.6 Learning from information security incidents
13.2.3 Collection of evidence	16.1.7 Collection of evidence
14 Business continuity management	
14.1 Information security aspects of business continuity management	
14.1.1 Including information security in the business continuity management process	17.1.1 Planning information security continuity 17.1.2 Implementing information security continuity
14.1.2 Business continuity and risk assessment	17.1.1 Planning information security continuity
14.1.3 Developing and implementing continuity plans including information security	17.1.1 Planning information security continuity 17.1.2 Implementing information security continuity
14.1.4 Business continuity planning framework	Deleted
14.1.5 Testing, maintaining and re-assessing business continuity plans	17.1.3 Verify, review and evaluate information security continuity
15 Compliance	
15.1 Compliance with legal requirements	

ISO/IEC 27002:2005	ISO/IEC 27002:2013
15.1.1 Identification of applicable legislation	18.1.1 Identification of applicable legislation and contractual requirements
15.1.2 Intellectual property rights (IPR)	18.1.2 Intellectual property rights
15.1.3 Protection of organizational records	18.1.3 Protection of records
15.1.4 Data protection and privacy of personal information	18.1.4 Privacy and protection of personally identifiable information
15.1.5 Prevention of misuse of information processing facilities	Deleted
15.1.6 Regulation of cryptographic controls	18.1.5 Regulation of cryptographic controls
15.2 Compliance with security policies and standards, and technical compliance	
15.2.1 Compliance with security policies and standards	18.2.2 Compliance with security policies and standards
15.2.2 Technical compliance checking	18.2.3 Technical compliance review
15.3 Information systems audit considerations	
15.3.1 Information systems audit controls	12.7.1 Information systems audit controls
15.3.2 Protection of information systems audit tools	Deleted

Table C: Comparison between ISO/IEC 27002:2013 and ISO/IEC 27002:2005

ISO/IEC 27002:2013	ISO/IEC 27002:2005
5 Information security policies	
5.1 Management direction for information security	5.1 Information security policy
5.1.1 Policies for information security	5.1.1 Information security policy document
5.1.2 Review of the policies for information security	5.1.2 Review of the information security policy
6 Organization of information security	
6.1 Internal organization	
6.1.1 Information security roles and responsibilities	6.1.3 Allocation of information security responsibilities 8.1.1 Roles and responsibilities
6.1.2 Segregation of duties	10.1.3 Segregation of duties
6.1.3 Contact with authorities	6.1.6 Contact with authorities
6.1.4 Contact with special interest groups	6.1.7 Contact with special interest groups
6.1.5 Information security in project management	New control
6.2 Mobile devices and teleworking	
6.2.1 Mobile device policy	11.7.1 Mobile computing and communications
6.2.2 Teleworking	11.7.2 Teleworking
7 Human resource security	
7.1 Prior to employment	
7.1.1 Screening	8.1.2 Screening

ISO/IEC 27002:2013	ISO/IEC 27002:2005
7.1.2 Terms and conditions of employment	8.1.3 Terms and conditions of employment
7.2 During employment	
7.2.1 Management responsibilities	8.2.1 Management responsibilities 6.1.1Management commitment to information security
7.2.2 Information security awareness, education and training	8.2.2 Information security awareness, education and training
7.2.3 Disciplinary process	8.2.3 Disciplinary process
7.3 Termination and change of employment	
7.3.1 Termination or change of employment responsibilities	8.3.1 Termination responsibilities
8 Asset management	
8.1 Responsibility for assets	
8.1.1 Inventory of assets	7.1.1 Inventory of assets
8.1.2 Ownership of assets	7.1.2 Ownership of assets
8.1.3 Acceptable use of assets	7.1.3 Acceptable use of assets
8.1.4 Return of assets	8.3.2 Return of assets
8.2 Information classification	
8.2.1 Classification of Information	7.2.1 Classification guidelines
8.2.2 Labelling of information	7.2.2 Information labelling and handling
8.2.3 Handling of assets	7.2.2 Information labelling and handling 10.7.3 Information handling procedures
8.3 Media handling	

ISO/IEC 27002:2013	ISO/IEC 27002:2005
8.3.1 Management of removable Media	10.7.1 Management of removable media
8.3.2 Disposal of media	10.7.2 Disposal of media
8.3.3 Physical media transfer	10.8.3 Physical media in transit
9 Access control	
9.1 Business requirements of access control	
9.1.1 Access control policy	11.1.1 Access control policy
9.1.2 Access to networks and network services	11.4.1 Policy on use of network services
9.2 User access management	
9.2.1 User registration and deregistration	11.2.1 User registration
9.2.2 User access provisioning	11.2.1 User registration 11.2.2 Privilege management
9.2.3 Management of privileged access rights	11.2.2 Privilege management
9.2.4 Management of secret authentication information of users	11.2.3 User password management
9.2.5 Review of user access rights	11.2.4 Review of user access rights
9.2.6 Removal or adjustment of access rights	8.3.3 Removal of access rights
9.3 User responsibilities	
9.3.1 Use of secret authentication information	11.3.1 Password use
9.4 System and application access control	
9.4.1 Information access restriction	11.6.1 Information access restriction

ISO/IEC 27002:2013	ISO/IEC 27002:2005
	11.6.2 Sensitive system isolation
9.4.2 Secure log-on procedures	11.5.1 Secure log-on procedures 11.5.5 Session time-out 11.5.6 Limitation of connection time
9.4.3 Password management system	11.5.3 Password management system
9.4.4 Use of privileged utility programs	11.5.4 Use of system utilities
9.4.5 Access control to program source code	12.4.3 Access control to program source code
10 Cryptography	
10.1 Cryptographic controls	12.3 Cryptographic controls
10.1.1 Policy on the use of cryptographic controls	12.3.1 Policy on the use of cryptographic controls
10.1.2 Key management	12.3.2 Key management
11 Physical and environmental security	
11.1 Secure areas	9.1 Secure areas
11.1.1 Physical security perimeter	9.1.1 Physical security perimeter
11.1.2 Physical entry controls	9.1.2 Physical entry controls
11.1.3 Securing offices, rooms and facilities	9.1.3 Securing offices, rooms and facilities
11.1.4 Protecting against external and environmental threats	9.1.4 Protecting against external and environmental threats
11.1.5 Working in secure areas	9.1.5 Working in secure areas
11.1.6 Delivery and loading areas	9.1.6 Public access, delivery and loading areas
11.2 Equipment	

ISO/IEC 27002:2013	ISO/IEC 27002:2005
11.2.1 Equipment siting and protection	9.2.1 Equipment siting and protection
11.2.2 Supporting utilities	9.2.2 Supporting utilities
11.2.3 Cabling security	9.2.3 Cabling security
11.2.4 Equipment maintenance	9.2.4 Equipment maintenance
11.2.5 Removal of assets	9.2.7 Removal of property
11.2.6 Security of equipment and assets off-premises	9.2.5 Security of equipment off-premises
11.2.7 Secure disposal or re-use of equipment	9.2.6 Secure disposal or re-use of equipment
11.2.8 Unattended user equipment	11.3.2 Unattended user equipment
11.2.9 Clear desk and clear screen policy	11.3.3 Clear desk and clear screen policy
12 Operations security	
12.1 Operational procedures and responsibilities	
12.1.1 Documented operating procedures	10.1.1 Documented operating procedures
12.1.2 Change management	10.1.2 Change management
12.1.3 Capacity management	10.3.1 Capacity management
12.1.4 Separation of development, testing and operational environments	10.1.4 Separation of development, test and operational facilities
12.2 Protection from malware	
12.2.1 Controls against malware	10.4.1 Controls against malicious code
12.3 Backup	
12.3.1 Information backup	10.5.1 Information back-up

ISO/IEC 27002:2013	ISO/IEC 27002:2005
12.4 Logging and monitoring	
12.4.1 Event logging	10.10.1 Audit logging
12.4.2 Protection of log information	10.10.3 Protection of log information
12.4.3 Administrator and operator logs	10.10.4 Administrator and operator logs
12.4.4 Clock synchronization	10.10.6 Clock synchronization
12.5 Control of operational software	
12.5.1 Installation of software on operational systems	12.4.1 Control of operational software
12.6 Technical vulnerability management	
12.6.1 Management of technical vulnerabilities	12.6.1 Control of technical vulnerabilities
12.6.2 Restrictions on software installation	New control
12.7 Information systems audit considerations	
12.7.1 Information systems audit controls	15.3.1 Information systems audit controls
13 Communications security	
13.1 Network security management	
13.1.1 Network controls	10.6.1 Network controls 11.4.3 Equipment identification in networks
13.1.2 Security of network services	10.6.2 Security of network services
13.1.3 Segregation in networks	11.4.5 Segregation in networks
13.2 Information transfer	

ISO/IEC 27002:2013	ISO/IEC 27002:2005
13.2.1 Information transfer policies and procedures	10.8.1 Information exchange policies and procedures
13.2.2 Agreements on information transfer	10.8.2 Exchange agreement
13.2.3 Electronic messaging	10.8.4 Electronic messaging
13.2.4 Confidentiality or nondisclosure agreements	6.1.5 Confidentiality agreements
14 System acquisition, development and maintenance	
14.1 Security requirements of information systems	
14.1.1 Information security requirements analysis and specification	12.1.1 Security requirements analysis and specification
14.1.2 Securing application services on public networks	10.9.1 Electronic commerce
14.1.3 Protecting application services transactions	10.9.2 On-line transactions
14.2 Security in development and support processes	
14.2.1 Secure development policy	New control
14.2.2 System change control procedures	12.5.1 Change control procedures
14.2.3 Technical review of applications after operating platform changes	12.5.2 Technical review of applications after operating system changes
14.2.4 Restrictions on changes to software packages	12.5.3 Restrictions on changes to software packages
14.2.5 Secure system engineering principles	New control
14.2.6 Secure development environment	New control

ISO/IEC 27002:2013	ISO/IEC 27002:2005
14.2.7 Outsourced development	12.5.5 Outsourced software development
14.2.8 System security testing	New control
14.2.9 System acceptance testing	10.3.2 System acceptance
14.3 Test data	
14.3.1 Protection of test data	12.4.2 Protection of system test data
15 Supplier relationships	
15.1 Information security in supplier relationships	
15.1.1 Information security policy for supplier relationships	New control
15.1.2 Addressing security within supplier agreements	6.2.3 Addressing security in third party agreements
15.1.3 Information and communication technology supply chain	New control
15.2 Supplier service delivery management	
15.2.1 Monitoring and review of supplier services	10.2.1 Service delivery 10.2.2 Monitoring and review of third party services
15.2.2 Managing changes to supplier services	10.2.3 Managing changes to third party services
16 Information security incident management	
16.1 Management of information security incidents and improvements	
16.1.1 Responsibilities and procedures	13.2.1 Responsibilities and procedures

ISO/IEC 27002:2013	ISO/IEC 27002:2005
16.1.2 Reporting information security events	13.1.1 Reporting information security events
16.1.3 Reporting information security weaknesses	13.1.2 Reporting security weaknesses
16.1.4 Assessment of and decision on information security events	New control
16.1.5 Response to information security incidents	New control
16.1.6 Learning from information security incidents	13.2.2 Learning from information security incidents
16.1.7 Collection of evidence	13.2.3 Collection of evidence
17 Information security aspects of business continuity management	
17.1 Information security continuity	
17.1.1 Planning information security continuity	14.1.1 Including information security in the business continuity management process
17.1.2 Implementing information security continuity	14.1.3 Developing and implementing continuity plans including information security
17.1.3 Verify, review and evaluate information security continuity	New control
17.2 Redundancies	
17.2.1 Availability of information processing facilities	New control
18 Compliance	
18.1 Compliance with legal and contractual requirements	
18.1.1 Identification of applicable legislation and contractual requirements	15.1.1 Identification of applicable legislation

ISO/IEC 27002:2013	ISO/IEC 27002:2005
18.1.2 Intellectual property rights	15.1.2 Intellectual property rights (IPR)
18.1.3 Protection of records	15.1.3 Protection of organizational records
18.1.4 Privacy and protection of personally identifiable information	15.1.4 Data protection and privacy of personal information
18.1.5 Regulation of cryptographic controls	15.1.6 Regulation of cryptographic controls
18.2 Information security reviews	
18.2.1 Independent review of information security	6.1.8 Independent review of information security
18.2.2 Compliance with security policies and standards	15.2.1 Compliance with security policies and standards
18.2.3 Technical compliance review	15.2.2 Technical compliance checking